THE GOOD SAMARITAN

**TOUCHSTONE
TEXTS**

Stephen B. Chapman, Series Editor

THE GOOD SAMARITAN

Luke 10 for the Life of the Church

EMERSON B. POWERY

Baker Academic
a division of Baker Publishing Group
Grand Rapids, Michigan

© 2022 by Emerson B. Powery

Published by Baker Academic
a division of Baker Publishing Group
PO Box 6287, Grand Rapids, MI 49516-6287
www.bakeracademic.com

Printed in the United States of America

Library of Congress Cataloging-in-Publication Data
Names: Powery, Emerson B., author.
Title: The good samaritan : Luke 10 for the life of the church / Emerson B. Powery.
Description: Grand Rapids, Michigan : Baker Academic, a division of Baker Publishing
    Group, [2022] | Series: Touchstone texts | Includes bibliographical references and
    indexes.
Identifiers: LCCN 2021034160 | ISBN 9781540960665 (cloth) | ISBN 9781493432516
    (ebook) | ISBN 9781493432523 (pdf)
Subjects: LCSH: Good Samaritan (Parable)
Classification: LCC BT378.G6 P69 2022 | DDC 226.8/06—dc23
LC record available at https://lccn.loc.gov/2021034160

Baker Publishing Group publications use paper produced from sustainable forestry practices and post-consumer waste whenever possible.

22   23   24   25   26   27   28   7   6   5   4   3   2   1

I dedicate this book to those good Samaritans whose kind acts
—especially toward people with whom they might disagree—
have caused them to alter their thinking
and maybe even their theologies.
May our imaginations be renewed!

Contents

Series Preface

In writing workshops, "touchstone texts" are high-quality writing samples chosen to illustrate teaching points about compositional techniques, genre conventions, and literary style. Touchstone texts are models that continually repay close analysis. The Christian church likewise possesses core scriptural texts to which it returns, again and again, for illumination and guidance.

In this series, leading biblical scholars explore a selection of biblical touchstone texts from both the Old Testament and the New Testament. Individual volumes feature theological *exposition*. To exposit a biblical text means to set forth the sense of the text in an insightful and compelling fashion while remaining sensitive to its interpretive challenges, potential misunderstandings, and practical difficulties. An expository approach interprets the biblical text as a word of God to the church and prioritizes its applicability for preaching, instruction, and the life of faith. It maintains a focus primarily on the biblical text in its received canonical form, rather than engaging in historical reconstruction as an end in itself (whether of the events behind the text or the text's literary formation). It listens to individual texts in concert with the rest of the biblical canon.

Each volume in this series seeks to articulate the plain sense of a well-known biblical text by what Aquinas called "attending to the way the words go" (*salva litterae circumstantia*). Careful exegesis is pursued either phrase by phrase or section by section (depending on the biblical text's length and genre). Authors discuss exegetical, theological, and pastoral concerns in combination rather than as discrete moves or units. They offer constructive interpretations that aim to transcend denominational boundaries. They consider the use of these biblical texts in current church practice (including the lectionary) as well as church history. The goal of the series is to model expositional interpretation and thereby equip Christian pastors and teachers to employ biblical texts knowledgeably and effectively within an ecclesial setting.

Texts were chosen for inclusion partly in consultation with the authors of the series. An effort was made to select texts that are representative of various biblical genres and address different facets of the Christian life (e.g., faith, blessing, morality, worship, prayer, mission, hope). These touchstone texts are all widely used in homiletics and catechesis. They are deserving of fresh expositions that enable them to speak anew to the contemporary church and its leaders.

Stephen B. Chapman
Series Editor

Acknowledgments

I dedicate this book to those good Samaritans whose actions have changed them. I'd like to mention the various people who have—in one way or another—impacted my thinking as this project developed. Living with a parable over several years encourages a lot of interesting conversations. Living with a parable as popular as that of the good Samaritan brings numerous opinions about its meaning. I wish this book could have included more of these engaging ideas about this first-century fictional story that has clearly shaped the lives and thinking and practices of contemporary people inside and outside the church in many ways.

I am grateful for the opportunities I have had to share segments of this research at Moravian Theological Seminary, Dubuque Theological Seminary, and Western Theological Seminary. The invitations from Dean Frank Crouch and Professor Travis West, respectively, were gifts, and the conversations that ensued were welcoming and warm. The COVID-19 pandemic hindered some opportunities, even as Zoom opened up alternative ones. I am grateful to local congregations that took advantage of these Zoom conversations, with several hospitable invitations from David True and Kathy Hettinga.

I have also been refreshed by many informal conversations along the way. For many years Jean Corey and I have walked into each other's classrooms at Messiah University to discuss the nature of reading—she, with Langston Hughes's poem "Theme for English B" by her side, and I, with Luke 10 in hand. Our efforts always encouraged my thinking, especially when they provoked our students. "How do you read?" (Luke 10:26) has become a constant query in my teaching due to these public encounters over the last two decades.

Others should also be mentioned, if ever so briefly. A fortuitous two-hour conversation with Cheryl Kirk-Duggan urged me to continue the work. Randy Bailey's timely phone conversations brought much-needed laughter even as we opened up new ways to think through "old" interpretations. Michael Fuller's reviews were always judicious.

Other colleagues closer to home should also be acknowledged. I appreciate my colleagues in the Department of Biblical, Religious and Philosophical Studies. I am especially grateful for the many conversations with Brian Smith, our department chair, surrounding various biblical phrases, ideas, or methods and for his understanding when I had to miss meetings. Drew Hart's presence and energy have been contagious, and our conversations always leave me more energized for the journey.

I appreciate the leadership at Messiah University—President Kim Phipps, Provost Randy Basinger, and Dean Peter Powers—for their continual support. The sabbatical granted in the fall of 2019 provided key months to focus on much of the research that went directly into this book project. The space that Lancaster Theological Seminary provided—both physically and spiritually—was timely and opportune. I am grateful to LTS's former vice president and academic dean, David Mellott, who negotiated this appointment; for the many kindnesses I received during my semester on the campus, especially from (former) President Carol Lytch, Greg Carey, Julia O'Brien, Myka Kennedy Stephens, and Catherine Williams; and for several meaningful conversations with David's successor, Vanessa Lovelace.

The Good Samaritan: Luke 10 for the Life of the Church has become a much clearer book due to the engaged efforts of series editor

Stephen Chapman and project editor Jennifer Hale Koenes. Their attention to detail and insightful questions forced me to rethink (and often revise) several areas of the project. Please know that any confusion that remains is due to my own stubbornness.

As Langston Hughes echoes in my head, so I hope he will echo in yours:

> So will my page be colored that I write?
> Being me, it will not be white.[1]

---

1. Hughes, "Theme for English B."

Abbreviations

Old Testament

Gen.	Genesis	Eccles.	Ecclesiastes
Exod.	Exodus	Song	Song of Songs
Lev.	Leviticus	Isa.	Isaiah
Num.	Numbers	Jer.	Jeremiah
Deut.	Deuteronomy	Lam.	Lamentations
Josh.	Joshua	Ezek.	Ezekiel
Judg.	Judges	Dan.	Daniel
Ruth	Ruth	Hosea	Hosea
1 Sam.	1 Samuel	Joel	Joel
2 Sam.	2 Samuel	Amos	Amos
1 Kings	1 Kings	Obad.	Obadiah
2 Kings	2 Kings	Jon.	Jonah
1 Chron.	1 Chronicles	Mic.	Micah
2 Chron.	2 Chronicles	Nah.	Nahum
Ezra	Ezra	Hab.	Habakkuk
Neh.	Nehemiah	Zeph.	Zephaniah
Esther	Esther	Hag.	Haggai
Job	Job	Zech.	Zechariah
Ps(s).	Psalm(s)	Mal.	Malachi
Prov.	Proverbs		

New Testament

Matt.	Matthew	Acts	Acts
Mark	Mark	Rom.	Romans
Luke	Luke	1 Cor.	1 Corinthians
John	John	2 Cor.	2 Corinthians

Gal.	Galatians	Heb.	Hebrews
Eph.	Ephesians	James	James
Phil.	Philippians	1 Pet.	1 Peter
Col.	Colossians	2 Pet.	2 Peter
1 Thess.	1 Thessalonians	1 John	1 John
2 Thess.	2 Thessalonians	2 John	2 John
1 Tim.	1 Timothy	3 John	3 John
2 Tim.	2 Timothy	Jude	Jude
Titus	Titus	Rev.	Revelation
Philem.	Philemon		

General

b.	born	e.g.	*exempli gratia*, for example
BLM	Black Lives Matter	Gk.	Greek
ca.	*circa*, about, approximately	i.e.	*id est*, that is
		p(p).	page(s)
cf.	*confer*, compare	r.	reigned
chap(s).	chapter(s)	s.v.	*sub verbo*, under the word
d.	died	v(v).	verse(s)

Bible Versions

CEB	Common English Bible	NIV	New International Version
ESV	English Standard Version	NRSV	New Revised Standard Version
KJV	King James Version		

Old Testament Apocrypha

Jdt.	Judith	Pss. Sol.	Psalms of Solomon
2 Macc.	2 Maccabees	Sir.	Sirach

Josephus

Ant.	*Jewish Antiquities*	*J.W.*	*Jewish War*

Bibliographic

BDAG   Frederick W. Danker, Walter Bauer, William F. Arndt, and F. Wilbur Gingrich. *A Greek-English Lexicon of the New Testament and Other Early Christian Literature*. 3rd ed. Chicago: University of Chicago Press, 2000.

The Preamble

This short book is about one of Jesus's most memorable parables, the so-called parable of the good Samaritan. It is also a book about the nature of interpretation: how different interpreters have engaged the wisdom of this first-century Jewish teacher. It is not, however, a step-by-step guide on the proper ways to understand ancient biblical parables. Rather, it will provide descriptions of various engagements with the parable and trust its readers to make their own interpretive judgments about what works and what may not. Within these pages, attention will be given to history, culture, linguistics, context, recontextualization, hermeneutics, ethics, and much more.

Many of these categories lie behind the (acknowledged and unacknowledged) assumptions interpreters make whenever they engage the parables of Jesus, which are imaginative stories that come to our age from a different time and place with their own cultural, religious, and sociopolitical assumptions about people, prejudices, and power. But these assumptions also come to us through tradition; our churches, our families, our communities have handed down insights into these stories that travel alongside the accounts themselves. Interpretive forces and assumptions are at work when these multiple worlds collide. The contemporary interpreter must decide whether the necessary goal is to get the meaning right or to enjoy the journey (although these are not necessarily mutually exclusive), hopefully with conversation partners in a community of others longing for and imagining a better world toward which we must work even in our short lifetimes on planet Earth.

It would be fitting then, in light of the title of the book, to begin with a retelling of Jesus's great parable, which is recorded only in Luke's Gospel (chap. 10).

A lawyer approaches Jesus—who is in a celebratory mood (vv. 21–24)—to probe about a particular concern: eternal life. Readers are aware that it is a test. Regardless, Jesus turns the question into a discussion about Torah: "How do you read?" (v. 26). This is a game two law interpreters know how to play well. Jesus acknowledges as much: "You have given the right answer" (v. 28). Then the tension in the story rises. According to Luke, the lawyer wants to "justify himself," so the game turns serious: "Who is my neighbor?" (v. 29).

To love a neighbor requires clarification because contexts, circumstances, relationships, laws, and a multiplicity of other factors have bearing on how people might interact with others. Who the neighbor might be was (and is) a good ethical and religious question. Jesus answers with the parable.

The parable begins with a tragedy. An unnamed person is brutally beaten, robbed, and left for dead. Three unnamed persons pass by on that road. Each one is briefly identified: a priest, a Levite, and a Samaritan. The first two make no effort to assist the traumatized man. The third person stops and provides aid, including assistance that will (eventually, so it seems) lead to his full recovery. Apparently, the man's "trauma" (Gk. *traumata* = "wounds"; v. 34) requires long-term care. Explicitly, this stranger takes the brutalized person to seek assistance from others and promises to pay for the full costs of his care. The parable ends here.

Following the parable Jesus turns to the lawyer and asks the ultimate question: "Which of these three . . . was a neighbor?" (v. 36 NRSV). Apparently Jesus created his own test, this parable. The lawyer passes the test with the correct answer: "The one who showed mercy" (v. 37). Jesus's final word is a challenge to act in this way as well. This final word reframes the entire passage from a discussion focused on the object of love ("Who is my neighbor?") to a discussion focused on the subject of love ("Which of these three acted neighborly?").

This parable is a short story. Yet it has generated two thousand years of questions and commentary, not only about what the story means but also about what it means to read and interpret the parables of Jesus—indeed, even Scripture itself. In the pages that follow, readers will discover several examples of *how* this concise parable has functioned in various times and settings. May these examples cause us all to reflect even more carefully on our reading practices and our treatment of our neighbors.

1

Who Is My Neighbor?

Luke 10 for the Life of the Church

The subtitles of the books in this series make a declaration that the volumes will be "for the life of the church." That subtitle deserves a fuller (though brief) explanation. The statement itself makes a theological claim. Theology is thinking, speaking, writing about God. All Christians make theological claims, whether they would describe them that way or not. Some may say, "I'm just attempting to live out my faith." The "my faith" part is the theological substance of what a Christian is claiming to live out. So writers of these volumes hope to enhance the life—the living, thinking, believing—aspect of the religious community.

Equally significant to this conversation is the singular "church" that resides in this claim. Of course, since the prayer of Jesus (John 17) it has become commonplace to think of and hope for a unified church. Nevertheless, since the very beginnings of Christianity, as represented in our earliest documents (the New Testament), there have always been multiple churches of various expressions. So I, too, speak out of *one* of these church traditions and write this volume in the hope that it will benefit more than my local community. Even so, my local ecclesial community has an impact on the kinds of theological matters I write.

Frederick Douglass's Theology from Below

I begin with Frederick Douglass, who represents a theology *from below*. That is, Douglass and other enslaved people who held on to the God of Christian faith needed to have ways of thinking about that God that gave them a sense of well-being in the midst of the most trying and debilitating circumstances. They had a theology that mattered bodily. Some may not classify Douglass (and the black enslaved people he represents) as a theologian.[1] Perhaps he was not, in the classical sense of that term. But he was a deep, brilliant thinker, and he often thought about the predicament in which he and others found themselves in the United States in the pre–Civil War era, while also attempting to understand the consequences of life and movement and freedom and God and others. As many have recognized, Douglass penned his narrative in the spirit of Augustine's *Confessions*, which is considered one of the great theological treatises of the early church.[2] In Douglass's conception of the church, he stipulated that there were two types of Christianities represented in the United States. In his appendix to the classic 1845 memoir, *Narrative of the Life of Frederick Douglass, an American Slave: Written by Himself*, Douglass senses the need to explain his severe critique of the Christianity he experienced lest he be viewed as anti-Christian:

> I find, since reading over the foregoing Narrative that I have, in several instances, spoken in such a tone and manner, respecting religion, as may possibly lead those unacquainted with my religious views to suppose me an opponent of all religion. . . . What I have said respecting and against religion, I mean strictly to apply to the *slaveholding*

1. J. Kameron Carter labels Douglass "a proto-black theologian, a religious thinker of the emancipated self" (*Race*, 304).
2. See Carter, *Race*, 286.

religion of this land, and with no possible reference to Christianity proper; for, between the Christianity of this land, and the Christianity of Christ, I recognize the widest, possible difference—so wide, that to receive the one as good, pure, and holy, is of necessity to reject the other as bad, corrupt, and wicked. To be the friend of the one, is of necessity to be the enemy of the other. I love the pure, peaceable, and impartial Christianity of Christ: I therefore hate the corrupt, slave-holding, women-whipping, cradle-plundering, partial and hypocritical Christianity of this land. Indeed, I can see no reason, but the most deceitful one, for calling the religion of this land Christianity. . . . We have men-stealers for ministers, women-whippers for missionaries, and cradle-plunderers for church members. The man who wields the blood-clotted cowskin during the week fills the pulpit on Sunday, and claims to be a minister of the meek and lowly Jesus. The man who robs me of my earnings at the end of each week meets me as a class-leader on Sunday morning, to show me the way of life, and the path of salvation. He who sells my sister, for purposes of prostitution, stands forth as the pious advocate of purity. He who proclaims it a religious duty to read the Bible denies me the right of learning to read the name of the God who made me. He who is the religious advocate of marriage robs whole millions of its sacred influence, and leaves them to the ravages of wholesale pollution. The warm defender of the sacredness of the family relation is the same that scatters whole families—sundering husbands and wives, parents and children, sisters and brothers—leaving the hut vacant, and the hearth desolate. We see the thief preaching against theft, and the adulterer against adultery. We have men sold to build churches, women sold to support the gospel, and babes sold to purchase Bibles for the *poor heathen! all for the glory of God and the good of souls!* The slave auctioneer's bell and the church-going bell chime in with each other, and the bitter cries of the heart-broken slave are drowned in the religious shouts of his pious master.[3]

This is my starting point for reflecting theologically on the biblical stories of the gospel. I do not assume that there is a single *Christian*

---

3. Douglass, *Narrative of the Life of Frederick Douglass*, 118–19 (his italics).

theological perspective that all Christians share. In fact, the impact of the *Protest*ant Reformation has taught us otherwise. There are many expressions of Christian faith and a variety of theologies that accompany those expressions. Many Christians think of *the* Christian faith—in the singular—even while most of those same Christians recognize the variety among us. In reality, not only do diverse Christians have different faith confessions (e.g., what counts as sacraments), but they also live their lives differently (e.g., what counts as "sin"). My beginning assumption is *difference*—that there are differences among Christian practices and interpretations. This assumption has a direct impact even on the way I interpret the canonical Gospels. I see difference in those accounts as well, even theological distinctions at times. Many biblical interpreters share these assumptions. If this is how the early Christian movement began, then perhaps there is some benefit for contemporary Christians to appreciate more the diversity among us. In turn, appreciation for these differences can make us value our own particular expression of the Christian faith even more. I grew up in a church in which Communion (or the Lord's Supper or the Eucharist) was considered a sacrament (even though we practiced it only monthly). Now I attend a church in which we practice the Eucharist weekly. Reflecting *theologically* on these differences can become an interesting reflective exercise of engagement in the practices and beliefs of the faith and the historical traditions that have led to this moment.

On the other hand, the kind of difference Douglass raises is a difference that relates to the dignity of human beings. His discussion taps into the essential ways in which ecclesial practices touch directly on the practices of everyday living. It expresses the deepest connections between the life of the soul and the life of the body. In fact, a theology that distinguishes too neatly between body and soul obscures the *embodied* nature of the theological commitments a church makes. The theological test becomes straightforward, though complex: What difference does a theology make on the way Christ-followers live *in relationship to others who are not like them?*

For Douglass, examples matter. Defining Christianity as "pure, peaceable, and impartial" is not sufficient, since most (all?) Christians would *self*-identify their faith in this manner. So Douglass goes one step further to define the opposite of this characterization. These examples are specific and telling: slaveholding, women-whipping, and cradle-plundering. A "Christianity" that performs these practices must stem from an improper theology, an improper way of thinking about God and God's activity in the world. Untroubled by these practices, those who practice this kind of Christianity do not simply act inappropriately; their teaching (and theological system) remains silent on these matters. Or worse, it actually leads them in this direction, as many slaveholding theologians were led when they advocated for a proslavery Bible. As Douglass acknowledges, it is not possible to promote the spiritual practice of reading the Bible while simultaneously promoting illiteracy among some. It is not possible to advocate for marriage and deny others the benefit of this union. There is a disjunction between these theological claims and the manner in which they were endorsed. The disembodied nature of this slaveholding theological system may be captured best in Douglass's analogy: "The bitter cries of the heart-broken slave are drowned in the religious shouts of his pious master." What Douglass recognized earlier in his narrative is the theological teaching that denigrates the human dignity of black people.[4] Douglass's recent biographer, David Blight, portrays Douglass in the spirit of the biblical prophet Jeremiah: "Douglass not only used the Hebrew prophets; he joined them."[5]

Some may prefer to keep their ethics (how one lives) and their theology (how one thinks/believes) in more clearly distinct categories. But such were inseparable in Douglass's thinking. I follow Douglass on this point. If you want to see how "good" a faith community's theology is, watch how they live it out. If there is no direct link

4. For a fuller discussion of how the formerly enslaved interpreted the Bible, see Powery and Sadler, *Genesis of Liberation*.
5. Blight, *Frederick Douglass*, 228. See also 157–58, 187, 219.

between their thinking and their actions—for example, if a local congregation excludes people who do not love the way they do—then any language that implies that they are a "welcoming" church should be called into question.[6] There is something misguided in the theology they proclaim. This approach is crucial to how I will interpret Jesus's parable of the good Samaritan.

The good Samaritan story is one of the best-known parables of Jesus in Christian history and has significant relevance for every age. Followers of Jesus need to be reminded that mercy is a concomitant act of faith. The faithful practice mercy. Jesus's story, as recorded in Luke 10, emphasizes this point in a dramatic way by placing an "enemy" as the central hero of the story. Undeniably, sometimes we can hear the truth only when the storyteller overdramatizes the point.

To hear this story afresh, interpreters must recognize that this is an account about more than mercy. Saint Augustine allegorized the parable in order to relay the teaching of salvation encapsulated in these few verses. Martin Luther King Jr. upheld one of Jesus's central motifs—a neighbor must show mercy—before expressing his desire to move beyond the parable proper and imagine a world in which there would no longer be robberies on that ominous road. My particular interest in this famous parable centers on the hermeneutical nature of Jesus's initial response. To the lawyer's opening query Jesus replies, "How do you read?" Indeed, the way one reads the Bible defines and determines the way a person thinks about life. Hermeneutics (how one reads) and ethics (how one acts) are rarely separable. Jesus reveals how he reads Torah when he places one unlike his (Jewish) listeners at the center of the story and asks his immediate audience—and generations to follow—to "go and do likewise." How should the contemporary faith community read this story and react accordingly?

6. Carter finds Douglass's analysis of his own situation lacking theologically because of his focus on identity, which remains stuck in the gender trap of modernistic thinking; i.e., Douglass becomes "free" only when he emphasizes his "manhood" as a "self-made man." Carter helpfully offers an intersectional critique, not allowing race to obscure gender (*Race*, 287, 289, 293).

Toni Morrison, *A Mercy*, and the Good Samaritan

Toni Morrison captures the fickleness and fleeting moments of community in her ninth novel, *A Mercy*. The Nobel laureate's book exposes the challenge of living with a diverse group of people and how larger societal constraints limit freedom and human choice.

A Mercy begins with the sixteen-year-old Florens, who narrates her confusion over her separation from her enslaved mother, a confusion that will not be explained to the reader until the final chapter of the book. She finds herself in the care of Jacob Vaark—whom she calls "Sir"—a landowner who has unwillingly secured Florens as payment for a debt. (Jacob despises human bondage, so he interprets this business transaction as an opportunity to save an orphan.) When Jacob arrives home to a 120-acre plantation he has inherited from a deceased uncle, he hopes that Rebekka, his spouse, will warmly accept Florens, a child who is near the age their daughter would have been had she not died. He is mistaken. Rebekka's attitude is more neutral toward Florens than Jacob had hoped. But Lina, a Native American servant Jacob had purchased from the Presbyterians some years earlier, takes Florens under her wing. Joining this group is Sorrow, an intellectually disabled, racially ambiguous individual who has been traumatized by a shipwreck, and two white day laborers, Willard and Scully, who apparently have queer leanings. In a twelve-chapter story told through the internal reflections of various characters, Morrison sets this "family" in Virginia in the late 1600s, when "America" and "race" were intermingling constructions prior to nationhood.

Jacob's death—in chapter 3—changes everything. As it harmed so many during those times, smallpox takes his life shortly after the construction of a large home that required additional, specialized help. Rebekka survives her battle with the disease, but she refuses to allow anyone to move into the large edifice that Jacob built. The refusal to live in this dwelling is symbolic of the decreasing humane interactions among those who remain living, as the small diverse community slowly perishes as well. As Morrison puts it, reflecting back on her own work, "I wanted this group to be the earliest example of American individuality," but it does not last because there is nothing outside to hold them together—whether race, institution, tribe, religion, and so on.[7]

In the final chapter readers finally learn how Morrison settled on her title. Florens's mother explains what happened on the fateful day when she made a strategic decision to "save" her daughter. She was the enslaved property of a person who had taken advantage of her sexually since the beginning of her time on his plantation. Her "master" is the father of Florens's little brother—whom Florens had thought her mother loved more than her. Seeing her daughter developing into a young teenager, she knew what fate awaited Florens—she had noticed the way D'Ortega, the master, had gazed (with clear evil intentions) at her daughter's movements. So Florens's mother—who remains unnamed in the novel—explains her efforts to secure Florens an alternative living space. Her master had been in debt to Jacob Vaark. When Jacob had visited her plantation in Maryland, she had noticed how different he seemed from her own master. He did not look at her with any particular (sexual?) interest when she set the table, served the food, and cleaned up following the meal. Jacob seemed hardly to notice her at all. When she learned that D'Ortega was going to attempt to use them as human collateral, she schemed to have Florens receive Jacob's attention. Jacob's willingness to take her daughter became, in her mind, "a mercy." For a mother to participate (or to be forced to participate) in the sale of her own daughter becomes an ethical query about the whole structural system in which she—and her "owners"—find themselves.

Florens, on the other hand, never learns the truth.[8] This revelation is a burden the reader must carry alone.

7. "Toni Morrison Discusses *A Mercy*."
8. This event may be a judgment about acts of limited freedom. "Free" people make the best possible choices under the given circumstances at the time and in the space they find themselves, only to discover at a later point that it may not have led

What can we gain from A Mercy *for reading the parables of Jesus?*[9] Morrison's novel—indeed, her entire oeuvre[10]—is about the way we read a shared history and thereby understand one another.

The following may not be your experience, but it has been mine. Over the years diverse communities—ecclesial or otherwise—form, and then, sometimes due to a tragedy or sometimes due to the "natural" desire of (North American) people for movement or sometimes due to the (usually) white flight to the suburbs, these communities splinter and break apart altogether.[11] Contact among members of the group does not necessarily end with the banishment of the temporary community—though sometimes it does. However, what gives the community its vibrancy and collective energy dissipates, and thereby group members go their separate ways.

Of course, there are always those members who stand on the fringe of these groups, never quite belonging or not quite feeling comfortable. Morrison is a genius at capturing the internal struggles of individuals of "less" status. It is not only the characters "Sir" and "Mistress" who speak and offer their descriptions about the world and their feelings about a given situation.[12] Morrison also brings to the world's attention the voices often overlooked in democratic Western society's "great" novels. These so-called minor characters receive much attention in Morrison's novels as thinking, speaking, thriving people on their own, even when the circumstances of life

---

to the best possible future. A person with less freedom has fewer options and should be judged—if criticized at all—on limits that their contexts impose.

9. There are several potential gains: (1) the structure of the novel, in which many voices offer diverse observations; (2) the role of religious conflict; and (3) the ongoing journey toward freedom. In the text above, I concentrate my reflections primarily on the first two items listed here.

10. The most influential of Morrison's novels, to my thinking, include *The Bluest Eye* (1970), *Song of Solomon* (1977), *Beloved* (1987), and *A Mercy* (2008). Her theoretical work in *Playing in the Dark* (1992) is foundational.

11. "White flight" is a common enough practice in the United States that it has generated its own wiki page. See Wikipedia, s.v. "White Flight," last modified May 25, 2021, https://en.wikipedia.org/wiki/White_flight.

12. This is what Florens (the lead character) calls Jacob and Rebekka Vaark.

apparently dictate many of their actions. As Morrison describes her own writing life, writing has been about a journey for freedom. She imagines how her characters yearn for more human freedoms than a country's laws may grant them.

Morrison's structuring of *A Mercy*—which she says was the hardest part to organize[13]—is a way of interpreting events. Morrison offers a multivoiced approach to the narration, which is a helpful guide to seeing the world from many different angles, though it is at times challenging to read. She includes an interpretation of the world and religious institutions, especially through the voices of female characters. By virtue of the structure, in which Florens narrates every other chapter, Florens becomes the lead character of the story. The naming of the book, after all, targets an event that affects *her* life and future.

A Mercy also opens a conversation about the way religious thinking shapes people differently. The complicated gestures toward religion and the religious may also prove to be helpful analogues to reflecting on the ancient parables of Jesus.

The structure of *A Mercy* allows for the perspectival nature of religious belief and experience. As Mara Willard recognizes, "Morrison's polyphonic narrative structure tutors the reader in religious pluralism and subverts claims to exclusive religious authority."[14] Moreover, the setting of the so-called new world is a perfect setting for exploring imaginatively the fluency and tensions that arise with religious beliefs. While many religious individuals perform kind actions—a priest teaches Florens how to read, the (Baptist?) Separatists help Jacob build his second house, the Presbyterians take in Lina after the destruction of her village—equally problematic actions stem from the religious tensions people confront. The Vaarks' kindnesses toward others coincide with their detachment from the local religious community. Throughout the book, it appears the more "religious" people become, the less able they are to sympathize with the other,

13. "Toni Morrison Discusses *A Mercy*."
14. Willard, "Interrogating *A Mercy*," 480.

the stranger, the outcast, the Native American (Lina), the African (Florens), and the disabled (Sorrow). But the Vaarks welcome them all into their family, even if unevenly.[15] This spirit of kindness ends, however, when Jacob dies. Rebekka may have recovered from her own illness and from the deaths of three young children, but she is unable to do so after her love's death. In a manner that captures Rebekka's recovery of religion's focus on the soul but distrust of the body of the other, Florens describes the situation: "Each time she returns from the meetinghouse her eyes are nowhere and have no inside."[16] Despite her lack of any traditional ecclesial commitment, Morrison's Rebekka, as Willard points out, does what any seventeenth-century Reformed Christian would do and views her suffering as divine judgment and turns back to Christianity for salvation.[17]

Some reviewers criticize Morrison harshly for her portrayal of religious people in A Mercy and elsewhere.[18] Yet it is clear that, despite her evident criticisms, Morrison displays how "images with deep Christian antecedents inform the novel."[19] Lina criticizes the Vaarks' lack of commitment to any (religious?) community, Jacob understands his action to take in three young maidens as rescuing orphans, and Jacob also interprets his hatred for human bondage as a religious sensibility, even if other religious people (e.g., Catholics) do not share the

15. This subtle critique of religion and its practitioners may function as a contemporary literary analogy for Jesus's use of the "Samaritan" as the one who shows mercy.

16. Morrison, A Mercy, 159.

17. Willard, "Interrogating A Mercy," 473. In the narrative, after the unnamed African blacksmith announces that Rebekka will live, she immediately falls on her knees to pray.

18. So, Willard: "These and other vivid examples of the cruelty and sorrow that Morrison associates with religion can certainly be read to suggest an authorial judgment upon this world of Roman Catholicism, Anglicanism, and Christian Non-Conformism. Morrison fixes her readers' gaze steadily upon the violence and intolerance of Christians across the continents: slave traders, witch-hunters, sexually exploitative clergy, theologies of a vengeful God who communicates divine will through suffering. This is consistent with the author's work elsewhere" ("Interrogating A Mercy," 474). Also Stave, "'More Sinned against Than Sinning.'"

19. Willard, "Interrogating A Mercy," 476.

sentiment. What remains troubling for many reviewers is the broken community at the end of *A Mercy*.[20] This story ends with multiple loose ends: Florens never discovers why her mother participated in her sale (although readers are informed); Lina and Rebekka, once confidants, rarely communicate with each other; and Rebekka places Florens up for sale. This is not Morrison's *Beloved* for sure.[21]

Morrison wanted her books to contain the incomplete feelings that the African American spirituals represent. In her words, "I want my books to be like that—because I want that feeling of something held in reserve and the sense that there is more—that you can't have it all right now."[22] She accomplishes this goal with *A Mercy*. It may just be that Jesus's parables are like the spirituals too. We will pursue this general idea later. Unless readers, thinkers, and believers are comfortable with the inevitable gaps the spirituals allow, they will struggle with Morrison's novels and perhaps with Jesus's parables too.[23]

A Samaritan in the Middle of the Night

"Why," I asked Saul, "did you agree to take this man in? Do you not know that his presence could ruin us? We have a business to run.[24] Now you will be preoccupied with his care, or I suspect you will expect me to handle his care. If I'm busy doing that, who will prepare meals for the other guests?"

Those were my initial reactions when my husband returned from the brief conversation with the Samaritan stranger. It was odd enough that we

20. Stave, "'More Sinned against Than Sinning,'" 137.
21. See also Stave, "'More Sinned against Than Sinning,'" 137.
22. Quoted in Willard, "Interrogating *A Mercy*," 471–72.
23. Shirley Stave is more of an apologist for a traditional Christianity, which Morrison's characters criticize. Unlike others (e.g., Willard), Stave is unable to find any real appeal (or complexity) in Morrison's version of Christianity, which appeals to earthly acts of salvation rather than a desire for a heavenly pie in the sky.
24. After creating a number of these imaginative reflections—an activity I have used in teaching undergraduates but have not attempted to utilize in any formal publication—I was pleased to stumble upon Kathleen O'Connor's work with imaginative reflections as a beneficial exercise for thinking with stories in *Jeremiah: Pain and Promise*.

were allowing the Samaritan and his wounded friend to spend one night. In some ways we had no choice since it was so late in the evening when they arrived and the man on the mule was in poor shape. Even though I had been standing at a distance, I could see that the man's wounds were bleeding through the poorly wrapped bandages. What kind of Jews would we be if we did not let them stay the night!

When Saul had awoken early to meet with the Samaritan, I had assumed that it was to receive the final payment for the night's stay and to bid farewell. But after the exchange the Samaritan man had departed *without his partner* and without his animal. I was confused until Saul explained what was happening. I couldn't help but react: "Why did you agree?"

Initially, Saul attempted to calm my concerns: "Don't worry. The Samaritan plans to return in a couple of days."

I reacted again: "You can't believe that will happen, do you? You know how most people are, and this is a *Samaritan* stranger who came in the middle of the night!"

Then Saul told me about the man's promise to reimburse us for any expenses.

"Really?!" I said at the top of my voice. "You accepted a promise from this foreigner?"

As I turned and began storming out of the front room, I could hear Saul saying in my direction, "Whoever gives to the poor will lack nothing, but one who turns a blind eye will get many a curse."[25]

"Don't fool yourself!" I shouted back. "You're no King Solomon!"

The Good Samaritan and Contemporary Tragedy

The Amish Community at Nickel Mines

On October 2, 2006, Charles Carl Roberts IV walked into a one-room schoolhouse, took the lives of five young girls, and injured five others before putting the gun to his head and taking his own life. From Columbine (1999) to Parkland (2018), the United States has

25. Prov. 28:27 NRSV.

become accustomed to hearing of school shootings, but this central Pennsylvania shooting was distinctive because of the targeted group: the Amish community of Nickel Mines (Lancaster).

In a country in which school shootings have become frighteningly routine,[26] this story received extraordinary media attention because of the nation's interest in this lesser-known, more isolated community that many assumed would be insulated from such tragedies. They were not. As one Amish leader acknowledged, "This was our 9/11."[27]

Part of what made this story distinct from other similar tragedies was the communal response of the Amish community. The entire Amish community felt the burden of the loss of six lives and the physical injuries to several others. As is their practice, they reached out with their entire support network to the families most affected in an attempt to share the weight of the tragic loss of young lives.

Much more surprising to the general public was the immediate response of the Amish to the killer's family, a family not Amish but "neighbors" to the Amish. In fact, the shooter was a truck driver who frequented Amish farms to collect milk. Only hours after the devastation, members of the Amish community began to reach out to the family members of the killer—a spouse, three children, and others—sharing in their loss as well. "Unlike the Amish victims," Donald Kraybill, Steven Nolt, and David Weaver-Zercher observe, "the Roberts family had to bear the shame of having a loved one inflict such pain on innocent children and families."[28] The Amish shared food with the killer's family daily and acknowledged through words and actions that the family was not to be blamed for the individual shooter's actions; this provided a communal act of forgiveness. Years

26. CNN's database lists 180 school shootings over the past decade. See Walker, "10 Years." In addition, hundreds of active-shooter drills permeate K–12 schools throughout the country.

27. Quoted in Kraybill, Nolt, and Weaver-Zercher, *Amish Grace*, 17. Many of the details above come from this book.

28. Kraybill, Nolt, and Weaver-Zercher, *Amish Grace*, 43.

later, the two communities remain in touch with each other.[29] This act of solidarity is central to the book *Amish Grace: How Forgiveness Transcended Tragedy*, penned by three experts on Amish life. Despite the title of the book, the authors acknowledge that the Amish are uncomfortable talking about "Amish grace" because many of them believe "grace is a gift that God alone can give."[30]

In an interview about the book, one of the three authors recognized the troubling fascination the American public has with a speedy closure: "It seems to me that the extension of Amish forgiveness allowed observers who were disturbed by the violence to bring 'closure' to this senseless act of violence when in fact quick and superficial closure was not warranted. And the media was more than happy to provide their consumers with a 'happy' ending. I myself would have hoped for less closure and more reflection not only on forgiveness, but on the violence that occasioned the Amish response."[31]

The Tragedy at Emanuel African Methodist Episcopal Church

A few years later, on June 17, 2015, another senseless act occurred. A twenty-one-year-old white man went inside a church and discovered a Bible study in progress. He sat with those in the study for almost an hour (by several accounts) and listened to their reflections about faith and life as they attempted to make meaning from the biblical passage (the parable of the sower) they were studying for that evening. Dylann Roof eventually decided that it was time to do what he consciously planned to do when he entered Emanuel African Methodist Episcopal Church that Wednesday evening. He pulled out his .45-caliber Glock handgun and killed nine people at point-blank range while they were saying their final prayers for the evening. From the elderly (Susie Jackson, age eighty-seven) to the young (Tywanza Sanders,

29. Itkowitz, "Her Son Shot Their Daughters."
30. Kraybill, Nolt, and Weaver-Zercher, *Amish Grace*, xiii.
31. "Amish America Q-and-A."

age twenty-six), Roof made no distinction.[32] He simply wanted to kill African American people and, in his own words, start a "race war."[33] A few weeks later, Roof confessed in a journal entry, "I have not shed a tear for the innocent people I killed."[34]

It is as much for the wicked as for the innocent that grace abounds. Of course, it is one thing to write this down and to believe it in the abstract. It is another thing altogether to be directly affected—that is, to be harmed or even to have one's life circumstances completely altered with the loss of a loved one—and still be *willing*, because love and forgiveness is an act of the human will, to forgive the evil act of another. "I forgive you," Nadine Collier said to Roof, who took the life of Collier's mother, Ethel Lee Lance, on that fatal night. "You took something very precious from me. I will never talk to her again. I will never, ever hold her again. But I forgive you. And (may God) have mercy on your soul."[35] A sister of one of the deceased said in court, "We have no room for hating, so we have to forgive."[36] To put it another way, reflecting on another tragedy, "The acid of hate destroys the container."[37] These words of forgiveness—or the act of forgiveness witnessed in the Amish community—do not suggest that people whose lives are most affected by these violent tragedies *forget* the harm that has been perpetrated. How can they ever forget? The truth is much greater than that. These folks recognize that without forgiveness, the human mind, body, and soul cannot continue in this life in a healthy way.[38]

32. Sack and Blinder, "Heart-Rending Testimony." Also see Wikipedia, s.v. "Charleston Church Shooting," last modified May 19, 2021. https://en.wikipedia.org/wiki/Charleston_church_shooting.

33. Quoted by Barron, "Forgiving Dylann Roof."

34. Quoted by Barron, "Forgiving Dylann Roof." For Barron "forgiveness is the writing off of a debt." If so, must the perpetrator *receive* the forgiveness? In light of his understanding of Jesus's teaching, Barron would likely respond that "Jesus commands generous acts precisely toward those who cannot or will not return the favor."

35. Nahorniak, "Families to Roof."

36. Quoted by Barron, "Forgiving Dylann Roof."

37. As one Amish farmer confessed. Quoted by Kraybill, Nolt, and Weaver-Zercher, *Amish Grace*, 125.

38. Toussaint, Worthington, and Williams, *Forgiveness and Health*.

It is troubling (and very American) how quickly the forgiveness story superseded the violence story. Deep down I think it might be the better way—the more humane, even more therapeutic way—to dwell on the good rather than on the evil. Yes, I think this is the Amish way, the way of the members of Emanuel, and I believe it is the way of Jesus. What bothers and even frightens me is how much I agree with Weaver-Zercher's observation that we desire to move past the tragedy too quickly instead of reflecting more deeply and critically on *how* the tragedy happened, on the mental instability of individuals, on the access to firearms in our culture, and on how we have to do more nationally (politically) and locally (ecclesially) to combat these causes of violence. Violence does not simply happen. It happens because something deep down is wrong. Communal forgiveness expressed in acts of kindness should attract our attention. But it ought not hinder a deep engagement with how we as a society have come to this point. Furthermore, how we pass along these stories matters!

The Truth and Reconciliation Commission

Bishop Desmond Tutu wrote a book about his involvement in the Truth and Reconciliation Commission (1996) following the end of South African apartheid, titled *No Future without Forgiveness*. Denying the past is no way—in Tutu's words—to create a positive future. South African apartheid was a political system put in place by the National Party government in 1948 that included, among other things, the following:

- Only white people were allowed to vote; nonwhites lost voting political representation in 1970, and Asians were *never* allowed to vote.
- Races—formally labeled as black, white, colored (mixed race), and Indian—were segregated in all aspects of life, including housing and schools.

- Three and a half million nonwhite South Africans were removed from their homes and forced into segregated neighborhoods; many of these people are still attempting to recover their former properties legally.
- The government reserved most skilled jobs for its white citizens.
- Sexual relations between persons of different races were banned.

In 1994, apartheid ended with the election of Nelson Mandela as president of South Africa.

One of Mandela's first presidential acts (after becoming the first black democratically elected president in South Africa) was to form the Truth and Reconciliation Commission under the leadership of Tutu, a well-respected leader from the Christian community. The commission "received more than 22,000 statements from victims" who "gave testimony about gross violations of human rights," including "torture, killings, disappearances and abductions," the kinds of action not expected in any humane society. In addition to listening to testimonies, "the commission . . . granted 1,500 amnesties for thousands of crimes committed during the apartheid years."[39]

I am particularly intrigued by the idea and process of the commission. Crucial to the commission's underlying philosophy was the awareness that reconciliation is not possible without truth. Moreover, action must accompany honest confessions of truth that are shared in the public domain. Of course, forgiveness itself is not the same as reconciliation, but it is the first step toward reconciliation. In the cases in South Africa, the archbishop believed firmly that forgiveness (or political amnesty) was an essential act of reconciliation.

A type of partial amnesia has affected the racial situation in the United States because of the country's inability to hold a public commission like the one in South Africa. It is this kind of amnesia

39. Tutu, "Truth and Reconciliation Commission." One major critique of the commission—which even Tutu recognized—was its failure to deal with economic polarities in light of the "legal" allowances granted to white citizens under the apartheid system.

that leads to the societal racial injustices that continue to plague this country collectively, as well as the individual misunderstandings in many everyday interactions that lead us to the present experience that has called for the Black Lives Matter (BLM) movement and the public displays of protest from professional athletes. But as Tutu's work of reconciliation has shown, there is no future without forgiveness, and there is no forgiveness without honest confessions about the wrongs that have been done to one another.

Contemporary Tragedies and the Good Samaritan

What do we gain from these tragedies and acts of forgiveness? How are they similar to and different from the good Samaritan story? How might they *complicate* that story, and in turn, how might the biblical story *complicate* the way we view and publicly discuss the contemporary communal acts of forgiveness? Finally, what does Morrison's tale *A Mercy* have to do with any of it?

Although not acknowledged directly, the principles of the parable of the good Samaritan lay behind these Christian communities' responses to their tragic situations.[40] Of course, how the wider non-ecclesial(!) community reached out in both instances should also be remembered.[41] Acknowledging the wider community's proactive assistance, one Amish man confessed, "We were all Amish this week."[42]

Among the Amish were legitimate concerns about the schoolhouse becoming a frequently visited tourist attraction in central Pennsylvania. Furthermore, the Amish were concerned about the children who

40. It is appropriate to try to avoid what Weaver-Zercher calls "the domestication of the Amish," even as I attempt to use the Amish as a contemporary example of Jesus's words. As Weaver-Zercher points out, "Rather than seeing the Amish for what they are—twenty-first century Americans who have chosen a challenging path of cultural resistance—the Amish are seen as people who have maintained a lifestyle from another time and represent the imagined values of that bygone era. This is what I call the domestication of the Amish. In my view, the Amish are much more radical than that." See "Amish America Q-and-A."

41. Kraybill, Nolt, and Weaver-Zercher, *Amish Grace*, 29–42.

42. Kraybill, Nolt, and Weaver-Zercher, *Amish Grace*, 31.

would be "reminded of the terror of that hour, day after day, season after season, as they sat in the room where five of their peers had died and another five were wounded."[43] Might the Amish response to raze the schoolhouse ten days after the shooting be an appropriate analogy to Martin Luther King Jr.'s sermon on tearing up the "Jericho Road" on which the innocent are brutalized?[44]

Many contemporary Christians privilege an interpretation of the Luke 10 passage that equates the good Samaritan with Jesus. Sitting in a Barnes & Noble while reflecting on this chapter, I overheard this interpretation from a neighboring table. It is understandable why contemporary readers prefer this interpretation. It is even spiritually edifying to see Jesus as the one who cares for us, bandages us up, places us in his immediate care, and transports us to safety (perhaps to the care of the church). This interpretive viewpoint has a long, rich history in the Christian tradition.[45]

The contemporary individualistic focus that shifts the story to include "us," however, fails to grapple with or account for what might be the most critical element of Jesus's story: his choice to imagine a hero his audience would strongly reject. That element seems as crucial to the story as the act of kindness depicted within the story. Indeed, the lawyer responds to Jesus's final inquiry with a reply that closes out the account: "the one who showed mercy" (Luke 10:37). The lawyer clearly recognizes what is, in his mind, the irony: the one who is least likely to stop and provide help is the one who did and thereby becomes the one classified as the true neighbor.

The parable of the good Samaritan has a history that is similar to a Morrison novel: there are many different angles on the story and thus many interpreters who express distinct views on Jesus's parable that generally reveal much about the interpreters' own cultural spaces

43. Kraybill, Nolt, and Weaver-Zercher, *Amish Grace*, 40.

44. Kraybill, Nolt, and Weaver-Zercher, *Amish Grace*, 40–41. Cf. King, *Where Do We Go From Here*, 198–99. The destruction of state or private property should not be equated with the loss of innocent lives.

45. Including Clement of Alexandria and Origen (cited in Gowler, *Parables after Jesus*, 34–35).

and times. Notice, for example, how many Good Samaritan Laws exist in the United States, a land in which a law is necessary to enable individuals to act in a helpful way toward a stranger in the middle of a crisis. It is not that most people would refuse to assist a stranger in need—though some might within our individualistic society—but a law is necessary to protect the "good Samaritan" from a lawsuit in case the act of kindness goes awry. It is the litigious society in which we find ourselves that is responsible for this kind of law, not the parable itself. To hear this story afresh—which is difficult to do with well-worn, often-told biblical parables—interpreters must recognize that this account is about more than mercy. By listening to others who utilize the parable in different contexts and as we engage a variety of perspectives in chapter 2, we will hopefully come to appreciate how much our own contexts shape the way we engage this story.

In that same spirit, Jesus's parable is not simply a story about one human being, a stranger, helping another human being. It is a story about the kind of community Jesus envisions for the world. The characters in his parable represent other groups—those people not part of the dominant group. In the Palestinian collectivistic society of Jesus's day, the culture rarely focused on the individual. That is clearly the case in this story as well. The cultural ethos of Jesus's day, especially in the Jewish communities in which he participated, is much more like the Amish community of our day than the generally individualistic settings in which most North Americans find themselves. So in light of this first-century cultural context, this parable may be a story about people groups and the myths that shape their perceptions of other people groups for later times and places.

What might this parable's teaching imply for the church? Several of the representatives discussed in chapter 2—Saint Augustine, Howard Thurman, the Solentiname community—have interpreted this story in light of the ecclesial settings in which they found themselves. So should we. Even then, we should not be surprised when churches with diverse theologies, practices, and commitments emphasize different elements from the story as key for emulation. For some of these church communities, this story will have bearing only on the ones who follow Jesus; for others, the story may have as much implication for the larger society in which the local congregation lives out its calling. Among the representatives discussed in chapter 2, Harriet Jacobs is the one who most clearly interprets the parable in light of the larger society's concerns. Jacobs interprets Jesus's parable in a nation that was debating what it meant to be free and who qualified for this basic human right. So, what might this parable mean for today's church? This parable (and our interpretations of it) may reveal as much about us collectively as a nation, as groups of people within that nation, and as individuals who inhabit various people groups as it does about the desires of particular followers of Jesus.

In the Samaritan's last words to the innkeeper, the story provides no certain closure. How long will it take to nurse the abused back to health? How much will it cost in time and money? If the man returns to full health, will he be able to return, eventually, to his prior commitments? Was he on a journey, and if so, to where? For what purpose?

The lack of closure in Jesus's parables is usually understated because the point the parable needs to make has been made: in this case, who the neighbor is. What remains is the undisclosed openness to human commitment to one another. It is a commitment that commentators and Christians alike would rather not discuss because their own respective journeys—similar to the Samaritan's—need to resume. Moreover, that resumption requires full attention. So the burden falls to the innkeeper. To put it briefly here, the Samaritan's act of kindness becomes a burden that others within the community must share. The Amish community and the community of Emanuel know this responsibility all too well. Communal commitment requires expectations of others when individuals make crucial, even life-altering, choices. When one person or group cares for another, when one person or group forgives another, when one person or group expresses explicit acts of mercy, then there is much more at stake for the larger community than the initial act itself.

It is surprising that some interpretations downplay the ethnic background of Jesus's hero in this story: the Samaritan. Part of the reason is a desire to locate ourselves within the story so that one of us can potentially become the one who commits the good act. The Samaritan becomes anyone. It may simply be the tendency of contemporary North Americans to ignore the ethnic category, even though it's a potentially crucial element of the story. Many white biblical interpreters would rather claim some "objective" perspective than recognize their own biases in their interpretive decisions. Morrison's thoughts on the absence of written reflection on the "black body" in white American literature may prove to be a useful analogy. As Morrison observes, contemporary liberals promote a "habit of ignoring race" as "understood to be a graceful, even generous, liberal gesture. To notice is to recognize an already discredited difference. To enforce its invisibility through silence is to allow the black body a shadowless participation in the dominant cultural body."[46] By noticing this absence, however, Morrison attempts to fill the void in her creative fictional work and pass along a more complicated "American" engaging story. In an analogous way, recognizing the ethnic identity of the Samaritan may provide insight into a more complicated biblical, ethnic-filled story that will, hopefully, speak more pertinently and radically to the present moment.

The Bible contains many stories about ethnic group interactions and ethnic conflict: from the Tower of Babel to Abram's departure from the land of Ur to travel to Canaan, from Israel's difficult departure from Egypt to their challenging entrance into Canaan, and from the Wisdom tradition's dependence on non-Israelite wisdom to the preservation of a book named after a Moabite heroine (Ruth).[47] Jesus's parable about this non-Jewish figure has many points of indirect

46. Morrison, *Playing in the Dark*, 9–10.
47. Many contemporary interpreters would rather focus on the non-Israelite character than on the Israelite preservation of this story, without which we would not have the story in the first place.

contact within the biblical tradition. We should not avoid Jesus's intentional choice of characters.

The characters of Jesus's story already have a shared mythic history. Jesus assumes that his audience shares a common sensibility about the ethnic conflicts that they, their families, and their villages have turned into living myths. These assumptions make Jesus's story work, allowing the structure of this story to gain traction and to provoke his audience.

I Will Always Love Ahab

I will always love Ahab, even if my parents forbid it. As far as I am concerned, Ahab is a Jew, but my family insists otherwise. I argue that he is a Jew because his mother is one; they insist that only a father's Judean ancestry can make someone a Jew.

"How could his Jewish mother," they swear, "marry someone from Samaria?" We go round and round until one of us storms out of the room. I know they will never allow me to marry him, but I will never love another.

I went to the market one day and overheard a rabbi telling a parable. Oh, it shocked everyone around me. I left immediately after he finished because I did not want to see or hear what the crowd was going to do or say to this poor-looking, traveling teacher.

The rabbi told of a person who was injured. I think he was beaten or something like that; I didn't quite catch the beginning of the story. It was clearly something the rabbi was making up.

In the story a priest walked by, and then there was a second person who also passed by the injured man. I'm not sure who it was. A lawyer maybe? Then, finally, a Samaritan was the third person to pass down this road, which piqued my interest. This Samaritan stopped and recognized that the man needed help, put him on a donkey, and took him to a local innkeeper a few miles away.

Get this! In the story, the Samaritan gave the innkeeper some money and told him that he would return in about a week and repay him for any other expenses he may have. A Samaritan did this—a Samaritan, one who has been harmed so many times by Jews like the robbers, by Jews like me. But in this story—in *this rabbi's* story—the Samaritan was the hero. Oh my, you should have heard the chaotic reaction to this Galilean teacher after he told that story. I had to get out of there before there was a riot—*over a story*.

On the way home, I thought about how much I wished this rabbi would visit my synagogue and teach there one Sabbath. I don't know if this way of telling stories is a common practice for him, but I would love to hear him talk more about how Jews should interact with others around them, whether they are Greeks, Romans, Barbarians—or Samaritans.

Hearing this story reminded me how much I love my Ahab.

2

The Good Samaritan in Christian Tradition

What You See Depends on Where You Stand

■ Augustine and the Good Samaritan: Christ as the Nonethnic Samaritan

> Augustine is one of the few thinkers of the Early Church who can be called "contemporary" to ourselves.
>
> Peter Brown, *Religion and Society in the Age of Saint Augustine*

Augustine and Place

Augustine of Hippo (b. 354), a bishop in North Africa in the fifth century CE (397–430), was one of the great writers, ecclesial leaders, and theologians of his day. Saint Augustine has become one of

---

I first recall hearing the common truism "What you see depends on where you stand" in the context of biblical studies from Elisabeth Schüssler Fiorenza. Others—as dissimilar as Albert Einstein to C. S. Lewis—have also said it.

the most remembered and thereby influential theologians in Western Christianity. For our purposes he was, most importantly, also an engaged interpreter of Scripture, partly because in the second half of his life he found within the biblical stories strategies for living a good life that were comparable to the contemporary philosophies he continued to study. However Augustine is to be judged today, he expounded on the biblical text because he assumed, rightly in light of his educational advantages, that many of the faithful (who were mostly illiterate) would learn written Scripture—and thereby God's voice—only through his teaching. Augustine fully believed that Scripture was generative for thinking and faithful practice.

Readers will have to turn elsewhere if they wish to gain a full understanding of Augustine's life, thinking, and influence on the church and world in which he lived.[1] My interest is more narrow—that is, to offer a brief exploration of Augustine's interpretations of the Luke 10 parable. By doing so, we will gain a formative construal of the Samaritan story that has stood the test of time and stamped its reading strategy—that is, Christ as the Samaritan—forcefully on the imaginations of the faithful in the centuries that followed.

As one who benefited from his family's support of an education that took him to Carthage and then to eventual teaching posts in Milan and Rome, Augustine's status distinguished him from many of the agrarian neighbors who frequently listened to his sermons and participated faithfully in the life of the community. In Augustine's day, attendance numbers were healthy in African churches, especially during special seasons like Easter and Christmas.[2] His parishioners' interest in faith was often an attempt to alleviate many of the social and psychological concerns related to the challenges of their economic context. As the great Augustine biographer Peter Brown

---

1. An excellent beginning point would be the classic introduction by Brown, *Augustine of Hippo*. A more accessible introduction to Augustine's thinking—albeit with a focus limited primarily to his *Confessions*—is Cooper, *Augustine for Armchair Theologians*. See also Stark, *Feminist Interpretations of Augustine*.

2. Chadwick, *Augustine of Hippo*, 71; Brown, *Religion and Society*, 17. See also Burrus and Keller, "Confessing Monica."

specifies, "We shall never understand the life of the towns of the Greco-Roman world unless we re-live, through the text, the creeping fear of famine."[3] As Jesus taught his first-century disciples to pray, so many believers in Augustine's North African milieu would also pray with attention to their contemporary reality, "Give us this day our daily bread." Despite this harsh fiscal context, in Augustine's interpretation the "robbed" man in the Samaritan story did not represent, surprisingly, those burdened by the economic challenges of his day. Finding the extent to which Augustine's interpretations were representative of the people of his age would require a much more critical study than this chapter.

Augustine and the Samaritan

The North African bishop was less concerned with the interpreter's method of interpretation than with the desires of the interpreter. To put it another way, Augustine was much more concerned with the outcome of a reading than with the particular details—though he shows a tendency for novelty. What should an interpreter hope to gain by reading the Bible? "Whoever takes another meaning out of Scripture than the writer intended, goes astray, but not through any falsehood in Scripture. Nevertheless . . . if his mistaken interpretation tends to build up love, which is the end of the commandment, he goes astray in much the same way as a man who by mistake quits the high road, but yet reaches through the fields the same place to which the road leads."[4] Or, again, "Follow this as a basic rule: that the text being read should be turned over and over, considered diligently for a long while, until your interpretation can be led over into the kingdom of love. If the text already rings true in the literal, then no figurative meaning needs to be probed for."[5] It comes as no surprise that Augustine provided multiple ways of interpreting the Luke 10 parable,

3. Brown, *Religion and Society*, 15.
4. Augustine, *On Christian Doctrine* 1.36.41.
5. Augustine, *On Christian Doctrine* 2.15.23.

always discerning for "the kingdom of love" he sought. Moreover, even if he could discover love through a literal approach, he would often utilize other methods if he could promise to extract more love for his listeners. Perhaps one of these methods is Augustine's attempt to go "through the fields," but both the allegorical and literal interpretations are presented below so that readers may decide which one provides more affection.

The Allegorical Approach

Augustine's allegorical interpretation of the Samaritan parable is one of the most popular examples of the method teachers use to instruct their students today. The following passage comes from his *Questions on the Gospels* (2.19), published around 400 CE:

> A certain man was going down from Jerusalem to Jericho. He is understood to be Adam himself, representing the human race. *Jerusalem* is that city of peace, from whose blessedness he fell. *Jericho* is translated as "moon" and signifies our mortality, because it begins, increases, grows old, and sets. The robbers are the devil and his angels, *who stripped him* of immortality, *and having beat with blows*, by persuading him to sinfulness, *left him half alive*, because the man was alive in the part by which he could understand and know God,[6] and he was dead in the part in which he was wasting away and weighed down by sins. And for this reason he is said to be half alive. But the priest and the Levite who saw him and passed him by signify the priesthood and ministry of the Old Testament, which could not be of benefit toward salvation. *Samaritan* is translated as "guardian," and for this reason the Lord himself is signified by this name. The binding of the wounds is the holding of sins in check. The oil is the consolation of good hope because of the forgiveness given for the reconciliation of peace. The wine is an exhortation to work with a fervent spirit. His beast of burden is the flesh in which he deigned to come to us. To be placed on the beast of burden is to believe in Christ's incarnation. The

6. Even after this tragedy, the human being had partial knowledge of God.

stable is the Church where travelers are refreshed from the journey as they return to the eternal fatherland. The following day is after the resurrection of the Lord. The two denarii are the two commandments of love that the apostles received through the Holy Spirit in order to bring the Gospel to others, or they are the promise of the present and future life. . . . The innkeeper, then, is the Apostle [Paul]. The extra expense is either the counsel he gave . . . or the fact that he even worked with his own hands, so that he would not be a burden to anyone in the newness of the Gospel.[7]

As creative as this approach may seem to the modern reader—"wine is an exhortation to work with a fervent spirit" rather than a balm with medicinal value in its first-century context[8]—allegory was a common cultural practice within a fairly stable interpretive tradition. Many of Augustine's predecessors (e.g., Irenaeus, Origen, and Ambrose)[9] would view Jesus's original story of the wounded body as a story about the human spiritual condition, one in which humans were lost, "weighed down by sins," "half alive," and in need of God's salvation. For them, the gift of salvation is impossible without the assistance of Christ, who not only comes in the figure of the Samaritan but also appears as the "beast of burden."[10] Even elements of the original story as apparently insignificant as the two denarii, which the Samaritan gave to the innkeeper as initial payment, take on figurative meaning as Jesus's teaching of the grand "two commandments" (love of God and neighbor) in this alternative reality.[11] Indeed, allegory was a method that allowed its users to equate the elements of one

7. From Augustine's *Questions on the Gospels* (2.19), quoted in Gowler, *Parables after Jesus*, 43. I left exclusive language in the cited passages, partly because of the complications of gender in Augustine's thought. See Stark, "Augustine on Women."

8. Or in our own day, symbolic for a quiet evening with a light meal and close friends. Augustine reports a story of his mother's (Monica's) predilection for wine at a young age (*Confessions* 9).

9. See Gowler, *Parables after Jesus*, 42.

10. Origen gave credit to an unnamed elder for the idea that the Samaritan was Christ; see Gowler, *Parables after Jesus*, 34.

11. "Love" does not explicitly occur in the Luke 10 parable, even if it is implied in the Samaritan's actions.

story with elements of another story, another reality, a reality that Augustine and his generation shared.

Not all equations, however, were worked out fully in the tradition. The two denarii offered interpretive options.[12] For Origen, "two" refers to "the Father and the Son."[13] The innkeeper offered allegorists lots of reasonable possibilities within the Christian allegorical tradition: for example, the head of the church (Origen), the Holy Spirit (Irenaeus), or angels (Clement of Alexandria).[14] Augustine's identification of Paul as the innkeeper may have been one of his most unique contributions to the interpretive tradition on this passage.[15] Augustine's preference for Paul as the caretaker of the inn might be explained by the fact that, as William Harmless points out, "Paul's letters shaped Augustine's biblical exegesis. . . . Paul's letters were his window on the Bible, his lenses for reading it, and he invoked Paul not only to resolve exegetical problems, but at least as often to articulate them."[16]

This flexibility within the allegorical method would be true about other elements from the original story for Augustine's contemporaries as well, even if there was an underlying shared understanding that the overall thrust of the story was about an alternative one: the story of God's plan of salvation, since all are reaching "through the fields the same place to which the road leads." In Augustine's case, Jesus's parable is the story of universal salvation in brief. Perhaps it is; it just was not the case for the first-century Jewish teacher. Augustine has to read against the grain of the text to explore his external story of spiritual salvation.

Before we turn to Augustine's second approach, notice also the key role of the church in the symbol of the inn within this interpre-

12. The first option—a reference to the two commandments of love—has bearing on the larger literary placement of the story; see Luke 10:27.

13. Cited by Gowler, *Parables after Jesus*, 34.

14. See Gowler, *Parables after Jesus*, 34.

15. Patrick Clark suggests that it was Augustine's most imaginative contribution in "Reversing the Ethical Perspective," 304.

16. Harmless, *Augustine in His Own Words*, 160.

tation.[17] While Luke's Jesus may have only a minimal conception of the role of the *ekklēsia* (church) in first-century Jewish life (the word never occurs in Luke's Gospel), he certainly understands the significance of the community for the gathering of God's people and the need for "neighbors," as his parable plainly delineates. The church, for Augustine, was the tangible place for working out one's salvation,[18] which was certainly true in Augustine's personal experience.[19] Augustine, too, understood his own life as this "Adam" figure who was on a journey to Jericho.

Following months of listening to the sermons of Ambrose, Augustine became gifted at interpreting biblical passages.[20] After his appointment to the priesthood, he requested and was granted a yearlong sabbatical to study Scripture, without which, he claimed, he could not serve the church.[21] During this time Augustine developed several methods for engaging the Bible. He used interpretive means other than allegory to make meaning available to his congregation. In the words of one scholar, Augustine "*spoke* Bible, making its words his words."[22]

The Literal, Moral-Example Approach

Most contemporary readers will feel more at home in Augustine's second approach to the biblical text. Augustine discusses this passage in his treatise *On Christian Doctrine*—a book that spells out his technique for how to teach Christian faith and includes the basic tools for interpretation of the Bible.[23] In a section in which Augustine wrestles with the question of whether angels are included in the concept of the neighbor to whom one should act kindly, he provides

17. For Augustine, the words of the Bible were signs with both literal and figurative meanings.
18. Cooper, *Augustine for Armchair Theologians*, 218.
19. See his *Confessions*.
20. Cooper, *Augustine for Armchair Theologians*, 94.
21. Cooper, *Augustine for Armchair Theologians*, 176.
22. Harmless, *Augustine in His Own Words*, 156 (his italics).
23. Chadwick, *Augustine of Hippo*, 82.

a retelling of Jesus's Samaritan story. In Augustine's world, how believers should respond to angels was a pressing issue; it was an age more superstitious than our own.[24] By the way, the short answer is yes, angels are neighbors too.[25]

Written around 400 CE, this discussion's larger context was, unsurprisingly, the theme of love.[26] In Augustine's brief retelling of the Luke 10 account (in italics below), he ignores the specific references to a priest, Levite, or Samaritan in an effort to make a more universal point: "Nobody was neighbor to this man except him who took pity upon him." Even then, his view of neighbor is more complicated than that.

> There arises further in this connection a question about angels. . . . But it is not irrational to ask whether in those two commandments is included the love of angels also. . . . *For when the man to whom our Lord delivered those two commandments, and to whom He said that on these hang all the law and the prophets, asked Him, "And who is my neighbor?" He told him of a certain man who, going down from Jerusalem to Jericho, fell among thieves, and was severely wounded by them, and left naked and half dead. And He showed him that nobody was neighbor to this man except him who took pity upon him and came forward to relieve and care for him. And the man who had asked the question admitted the truth of this when he was himself interrogated in turn. To whom our Lord says, "Go and do likewise"; teaching us that he is our neighbor whom it is our duty to help in his need, or whom it would be our duty to help if he were in need. Whence it follows, that he whose duty it would be in turn to help us is our neighbor.* . . . And, again, who does not see that no exception is made of any one as a person to whom the offices of mercy may be denied when our Lord extends

24. Chadwick, *Augustine of Hippo*, 88.

25. "It is manifest that the command to love our neighbor embraces the holy angels also" since they have performed many neighborly acts to benefit humans (Augustine, *On Christian Doctrine* 1.30.33).

26. In *Parables after Jesus*, David Gowler suggests that Augustine's emphasis on love is a notable feature of Augustine's interpretations of the parables (pp. 41, 44).

the rule even to our enemies? "Love your enemies, do good to them that hate you" [Matt. 5:44].[27]

Unlike in his interpretation in the *Questions on the Gospels*, Augustine did not allegorize the passage here. Rather, he acknowledged the ethical implications of Jesus's story on all followers: "teaching us that he is our neighbor whom it is our duty to help in his need." In addition, by ignoring the references to the Samaritan, Levite, and priest, Augustine avoided the cultural ethnic tension in Jesus's first-century story and thereby may have also ignored Jesus's challenge to fellow Jews to remember their own conflicted history with the Samaritans. Nevertheless, citing Jesus's words from Matthew 5:44, Augustine recognized implicitly the significance of the character roles when he attached this parable to his thinking on the "enemy": "Who does not see that no exception is made of any one as a person to whom the offices of mercy may be denied when our Lord extends the rule even to our enemies?" But he turned his exegetical antenna, so to speak, toward Jesus's teaching on the enemy rather than acknowledging the Samaritan as a potential enemy within the original story.[28] Augustine's omission of the Samaritan as a potential enemy to Jesus's audience may enhance another point he desired to contemplate.

By decontextualizing the original story in a manner distinct from his allegorical interpretation above, Augustine promotes a reading that invites his audience in a general way into an assessment of neighbors and enemies in their own world. Explicit allegory was not the only hermeneutical option available to accomplish this goal, even though some of the conclusions of that interpretive approach still lie behind Augustine's understanding here. As he mentions in an

27. Augustine, *On Christian Doctrine* 1.30.31.
28. Augustine's insistence on the Christian teaching to love the enemies "tended to undermine the military strength of the city and rob it of its most powerful defense against external foes" (Fortin, introduction to *Augustine*, x). It was no small imaginary exercise, as "some of Augustine's close friends had for many years refused baptism even after having been instructed in the Faith" (Fortin, introduction to *Augustine*, x). Such reasons as these provoked Augustine's publication of *The City of God*.

allegorical move a few sentences beyond the cited text above, Augustine thought that Jesus and the Samaritan character were one and the same: "For our Lord Jesus Christ points to Himself under the figure of the man who brought aid to him who was lying half dead on the road."[29] It is easier to draw this conclusion if one ignores the ethnic identity of the "hero" of Jesus's parable. How could, for example, the Savior be the "enemy"? But Augustine retains the moral requirement of the passage for Jesus's followers as people who should be simply following the actions of God: "For He [God] shows us pity on account of His own goodness, but we show pity to one another on account of His—that is, He pities us that we may fully enjoy Himself; we pity one another that we may fully enjoy Him."[30]

After all, the goal of interpreting the Bible is to love God more deeply and care for one's neighbor more faithfully.[31] For Augustine, love was God's gracious gift to humankind granted to assist them in finding ways to live more peaceably with one another. One story that so moved his passionate thinking in this direction was Jesus's great parable, a story figuratively about the great Jewish teacher himself. Indeed, one may assume that Augustine may also have thought of himself as another type of Samaritan, one engaged in the practice of teaching his neighbors, pouring on the oil and the wine to care for the souls of his parishioners. But since Augustine agreed with the allegorical interpretive tradition that Christ was the Samaritan, one option was to discover his own work in the symbolic counterpart

29. *On Christian Doctrine* 1.30.33. From the allegorical interpretation (addressed earlier), Augustine offered this explanation: "Samaritan means 'guardian,' and therefore the Lord Himself is signified by this name."

30. Augustine, *On Christian Doctrine* 1.30.33. When defining the neighbor, Augustine narrows the description: "But since you cannot do good to all, you are to pay special regard to those who, by the accidents of time, or place, or circumstance, are brought into closer connection with you" (*On Christian Doctrine* 1.28.29).

31. "Whoever, then, thinks that he understands the Holy Scriptures, or any part of them, but puts such an interpretation upon them as does not tend to build up this twofold love of God and our neighbor, does not yet understand them as he ought" (Augustine, *On Christian Doctrine* 1.36.40).

of the actions of the innkeeper/Paul for the inn/church. And so he did![32]

Augustine's Universal Appeal

Augustine's creative reading of Jesus's parable—for which there are many detractors—still has contemporary advocates who find in Augustine's approach to Scripture a view that may even now benefit today's Christians.[33] My intention is not to argue against the excess of Augustine's approach, as some contemporary biblical scholars do,[34] since I admit up front that allegory is another cultural method from another time. Each age brings its own concerns and approaches to biblical texts. Rather, let us acknowledge what some may find valuable from Augustine's interpretation while at the same time engaging some of the challenges it raises as a heuristic interaction with the biblical story.

Several interpreters find various aspects of Augustine's approach appealing: (1) The *christological* intention allows for a more universal appeal. (2) Multiple interpretations are available to the careful interpreter. (3) Love is the goal of any hermeneutical endeavor.

First, if Christ is the Samaritan, then Christ-followers should take his lead and "go and do likewise." This has a universal, rather than particular, quality to it. Furthermore, for Augustine, Jesus intended for the parable to be understood in this way in the first century.[35] It is not a secondary (allegorical, technically speaking) move for him. In Augustine's words, "If that interpretation remains hidden we should

32. This connection may be implied in Clark, "Reversing the Ethical Perspective," 304.

33. Many advocates come from outside of traditional biblical scholarship.

34. For John Dominic Crossan both of Augustine's interpretations are simply "wrong," since they misrepresent Jesus's and Luke's "original" intentions. Neither of Augustine's interpretations captures Jesus's original concern or even the original function of the parable (as a "challenge parable"); the neighbor in Crossan's interpretation of Augustine is both the aided and the one who provided aid (*Power of the Parable*, 52).

35. Teske, "Good Samaritan," 353.

certainly choose one that is not ruled out by the context of Scripture and that agrees with sound faith."[36] The "context of Scripture" for Augustine meant that the Samaritan represents a "guardian," and who else is our guardian than Christ himself according to the biblical witness? Some of us, reading a bit more literally, may choose to disagree with Augustine's sense of the "contextual" nature of a biblical passage, since there seems to be little evidence in the passage that implies Jesus's *intentional* association with the Samaritan. Of course, Augustine considered the whole of the biblical witness as "context" for any single individual passage. Contemporary biblical scholarship proceeds in a slightly different manner.

One defender of Augustine's universal appeal, Patrick Clark, explains it in this manner: "No longer is any ethnic or social characteristic sufficient for specifying the neighbor relation, but only the potential for acting in a way that would itself reflect and constitute the neighbor relation. This shift not only recategorizes the different identities in play, but ultimately decategorizes them in light of the moral injunction to 'go and do likewise.'"[37] Augustine's attempt to appeal to the universal is attractive to many. Jesus could have accomplished what Clark suggests by following a "traditional" parable procedure and labeling the third party a common Israelite (over against the Levite and the priest). That is what his audience would have expected, and it would have achieved a more universal point, one that any Jewish person could have lived out. Instead, the first-century Jewish teacher imagined a Samaritan. The particular choice matters.

Furthermore, as the narrative context dictates, Jesus may have imagined that a Samaritan did good in this case, but he did not explicitly imagine that he and the Samaritan were one. In fact, for Jesus the story would have worked more effectively if the Samaritan were *completely other*. Then Jesus and the lawyer would be placed on equal footing regarding the concern about neighbors. The difference

36. Augustine, *De Genesi ad litteram*, quoted in Teske, "Good Samaritan," 355.
37. Clark, "Reversing the Ethical Perspective," 303.

between these two law interpreters is how they might imagine the neighbor. The particular nature of Jesus's story, his imaginative exercise, emphasized the particular, the local, the regional, the historical figure in order to seize his audience's memory of the other. Moreover, the way that his audience is able to imagine differently their history together and their history with their neighbors determines how well they are able to live out Torah. The particular choice matters.

Second, Augustine did not advocate for only one meaning. He believed that many truths could be discovered in the rich collection of mysterious, Spirit-inspired literature.[38] As mentioned above, alternative interpretations needed to be supported by the "context of Scripture" or had to be in agreement with "sound faith," but how Augustine's understanding of the context differs from contemporary readings of biblical passages has to be accounted for. Unlike Roland Teske, Clark acknowledges the general patristic oversight of the ethnic identity markers of the characters in the Samaritan story—which seems so central to Jesus's creative work—"in order to draw from the text a meaning more expressive of universal doctrinal claims."[39] Multiple meanings may be derived from the same passage, but to accomplish this, sometimes "violence" has to be done to the original passage, including this act of narrative ethnic cleansing. In our global environment, the local (the particular) still matters.

Third, above all else, interpretation ought to lead readers to love more deeply. Ultimately, human love should be directed toward God. For Augustine, one way to express this action in bodily form is to love one's neighbor.[40] Teske expresses his defense of Augustine's approach in the following way: key for Augustine's interpretive objective was that an interpretation should reveal "Christ's loving mercy

38. As Teske puts it, Augustine "is equally clear that there are, if not always, at least often many true interpretations of a passage of Scripture" ("Good Samaritan," 355).

39. Clark, "Reversing the Ethical Perspective," 301.

40. According to Gowler, Augustine would have read the love connection into Origen's interpretation of the Samaritan story as well, even though for Origen the two denarii point to the Father and the Son. For Augustine, the two coins point to the twofold love commandment (*Parables after Jesus*, 34).

toward our fallen race and that his love for us provides the standard and model of how we should love one another."[41] With reference to this parable specifically, Clark argues that "Augustine's exegesis is not only reconcilable with the parable's moral confrontation of social divisions," but Augustine's interpretation "constitutes a natural theological outgrowth of the ethical paradigm that makes the best sense out of the actual narration of the parable."[42] That Augustine's reading "makes the best sense" is debatable. In Clark's attempt to privilege Augustine's viewpoint, he downplays Jesus's ethnic categories that explicitly call to mind the histories and memories of the relationships between the Samaritans and the Jews. Clark is nevertheless aware of the potential problems with Augustine's strategy: "Is Augustine's traditional allegorical reading ethically retrogressive?"[43] Clark's question captures well my concerns also, although I propose a different set of answers.

By turning the story into a divine-human encounter and away from Jesus's apparent aim, we may more easily ignore the embodiment of the ethnic dimensions of the human-human encounter. As a hermeneutical assumption, "love" may include or ignore the ethnic dimension. Some readers find the universal more appealing: "all lives matter." For others, to distinguish the ethnic dimension speaks to the absence of its recognized embodiment within the history of a society: "black lives matter." This latter confession does not disregard love, but it publicly acknowledges that love, too, sadly has a context. Not all have been loved in the same way. One's perspective determines whether one views the nature of the phrase as inclusive or exclusive. The so-called universal statement "all lives matter" may not be inclusive at all, at least from the perspective of the underside: "All lives can't matter until black lives matter too."

In the final analysis, we can benefit greatly from observing Augustine's interpretive practices. We should underscore Augustine's

41. Teske, "Good Samaritan," 357.
42. Clark, "Reversing the Ethical Perspective," 301.
43. Clark, "Reversing the Ethical Perspective," 304–5.

creativity, even though it belongs not to Augustine alone but to his entire age. Albeit in a different way, Jesus himself utilized the creative resources of the parable to imagine a different kind of world. In Augustine's period, there was a widespread belief that Scripture itself allows for, even beckons, creative interpretive moves within reason (reason = rule of faith). Scripture is "alive," and interpreters should mine it as such. We should also highlight Augustine's flexibility with respect to method. If one approach to the biblical text did not exhaust the potential meaning of a passage, other ways of looking into the words might produce additional signifiers. The North African bishop moved between methods to gain what was necessary for his larger objective. Finally, the larger goal of any interpretation was, for Augustine, the force of love, driven by the twofold command to love God and to love neighbor. Nevertheless, his creativity had limits. Nowadays we do not live in an era in which a rich allegorical tradition is able to communicate to others meaningfully. Augustine's flexibility has potential, but how should we respond to our modern multidisciplinary practices when results clash? Even though the emphasis on love as an objective is beautiful, it, too, has drawbacks when one begins to define the examples of that love. Augustine himself classified it as an act of love when he advocated for—with the support of arms if necessary—the forced reentry of Donatists into the Catholic fold.[44] When the *ethnicity* of hero characters challenges a group's ideas of lead protagonists, what might this say about the "rules" (of faith) a group has put in place?

Howard Thurman and the Good Samaritan: A Humanizing Tale

Let us now transition to Howard Thurman, another interpreter from another generation. For him the ethnic markers are central to Jesus's story and to his own. He exposes how Jesus himself—or the Jesus Luke portrays—imagines how the kingdom *should* be

44. Brown, *Religion and Society*, 278.

and discusses what it might mean in his own social and theological imagination if God were to be present in this human-to-human encounter.

Thurman and His Context

Howard Thurman was a minister, writer, professor, and mystic who also functioned behind the scenes as the "pastoral leader of the Civil Rights movement."[45] In the middle decades of the twentieth century, Thurman was recognized as one of North America's most influential ministers. *Life* magazine listed him among the twelve most influential religious leaders in 1953. *Ebony* magazine listed him among the fifty most important individuals in African American history.[46] He cofounded and copastored the intentionally interracial and interfaith Church for the Fellowship of All Peoples in San Francisco, arguably the first of its kind.

There are many fascinating stories worth retelling, but I will mention briefly only two because of their benefit in assisting us to grapple with Thurman's interpretation of the Samaritan parable. Both of these stories come from Thurman's autobiography, *With Head and Heart*, published in 1979.

During his years at Rochester Theological Seminary (now Colgate Rochester Crozer Divinity School, in upstate New York), he was profoundly influenced by a sentiment shared by one of his teachers, Dr. Cross. This professor advised Thurman not to waste energy on the social concerns of the day but to concentrate on deeper issues. Thurman recalls this professor's words: "But let me remind you that all social questions are transitory in nature and it would be a terrible waste of you to limit your creative energy to the solution of the race problem, however insistent its nature. Give yourself

---

45. Fluker and Tumber, *Strange Freedom*, 13.
46. Cf. Bennett, "Howard Thurman." Among his professional commitments, Thurman taught philosophy and religion at Morehouse, taught the Bible as literature, and served as a spiritual adviser at Spelman College. See Thurman, *With Head and Heart*, 78.

to the timeless issues of the human spirit." Furthermore, Thurman writes, the professor continued in this way: "Perhaps I have no right to say this to you because as a white man I can never know what it is to be in your situation." This advice struck Thurman deeply. Thurman apparently never replied directly to his professor, but the young Thurman thought to himself, "This man . . . did not know that a man and his black skin must face the 'timeless issues of the human spirit' *together*."[47] Thurman was, what we might call today, an "intersectional" thinker.[48]

From 1935 to 1936 Thurman traveled to India on a "friendship pilgrimage" and, among many other inspiring events, met with Gandhi. Along the way, his Indian hosts regularly challenged him, even calling him a "traitor to all the dark peoples of the earth."[49] He absorbed the pain from the charge: "Is Christianity powerless before the color bar?"[50] Thurman's reply insisted on a careful distinction between "Christianity" and "the religion of Jesus." The two were incompatible in his experience and in his thinking, an idea that taps into a long African American prophetic tradition of recognizing the difference.[51]

Thurman's 1949 book on Jesus, *Jesus and the Disinherited*, was a response partially to Dr. Cross and partially to the author's unnamed Indian inquisitors. Furthermore, Thurman managed to interpret the Jesus of the Gospels in a way that answered these concerns. In short, his emphasis on the Jewishness of Jesus allowed Thurman

47. Thurman, *With Head and Heart*, 60 (my italics).
48. "Intersectionality" is the recognition that a person or group may have more than one social identity (e.g., race, class, sexuality, religion, disability) that overlaps with another social identity, which may lead to a combination of factors that encourage discrimination against her or him. Lawyer and professor Kimberlé Crenshaw originated the term in legal circles in the late 1980s. See Crenshaw, "Mapping the Margins." More recently, see her TED Talk, "The Urgency of Intersectionality."
49. Thurman, *With Head and Heart*, 114. He devoted an entire chapter of his autobiography to this trip (101–36).
50. Thurman, *With Head and Heart*, 125.
51. See comments on Frederick Douglass's distinction "between the Christianity of this land, and the Christianity of Christ" in chap. 1.

to associate Jesus with all the disinherited of the world and thereby to interpret Jesus, his teachings, and his actions from that marginalized perspective.[52]

Jesus and the Disinherited *and Jesus's Samaritan*

In a way similar to Saint Augustine, Thurman discussed the Samaritan parable in a context in which the overarching theme was love. In a manner identical to Augustine, Thurman also found the twofold command—love God; love neighbor—as central to Jesus's teaching and as a crucial "survival technique for the oppressed."[53] But Thurman was more interested—at least on the literary surface—than Augustine in drawing conclusions about Jesus's conception of love in light of a first-century context and Jesus's close association to his own ethnic group.[54] For example, Jesus had to work out his idea of love (according to Thurman) in an integrated context in which non-Jews lived and worked among Jewish people. Following his trip to India, Thurman's fundamental question was on the relationship between Christian faith and the American context: "Is Christianity powerless before the color bar?"[55]

Beginning with a careful description of Jesus's first-century context, Thurman devotes entire chapters to each of the themes of fear, deception, and hate before turning his attention to an analysis of love. "The religion of Jesus makes the love-ethic central" is the opening sentence of chapter 5.[56] In Thurman's understanding, this central "love-ethic" is "embodied in the timeless words of Israel": love God and love neighbor.[57] It is a fundamental teaching of Jesus's community, Israel. As he thoughtfully lays out in the opening chapter of the

52. Thurman, *With Head and Heart*, 118.
53. Thurman, *Jesus and the Disinherited*, 29.
54. On Augustine's more positive view of contemporary Jews and Jewish customs, see Fredriksen, *Augustine and the Jews*.
55. Thurman, *With Head and Heart*, 125.
56. Thurman, *Jesus and the Disinherited*, 89.
57. Thurman, *Jesus and the Disinherited*, 89.

book, engaging the Jewishness of Jesus is vital for appreciating the first-century teacher.[58] Underlining the ancient ethnic and religious context of Jesus in the 1940–1950s of Thurman's world was much less common than one might imagine. In biblical scholarship on the historical Jesus, the rediscovery of Jesus's Jewishness was viewed as characteristic of the "third quest," a period dating roughly from the early 1970s on. An emphasis on Jesus's attachment to his Jewish identity would have been even less common in popular, ecclesial settings during Thurman's generation.

For Thurman, a mystic from the United States,[59] the good Samaritan parable provided initial and crucial support for Jesus's love-ethic. To explore the full meaning of love, Jesus had to develop the application of his love-ethic in light of the presence of the Samaritans, one group of "enemies" for Jesus's Jewish community. This imaginative story provides, according to Thurman, one explicit example of Jesus's cultural and theological thinking.[60]

As for the story proper, Jesus "depicted what happens when a man responds directly to human need across the barriers of class, race, and condition," as the Samaritan did.[61] With this imaginative story, Jesus defined the "neighbor" for the lawyer. In Thurman's more linear explanation, "Neighborliness is nonspatial; it is qualitative."[62]

For Thurman, the challenge of crafting a Samaritan as hero was extraordinary within the communal mores of Jesus's day: "This was not an easy position for Jesus to take within his own community."[63] Loving the neighbor required loving the group of "those of the

---

58. Thurman, *Jesus and the Disinherited*, 11–35.
59. For Thurman it was not incompatible to be a "mystic" (concerned with one's deep interior longings) and a social change agent: "The mystic is forced to deal with social relations because in his effort to achieve the good, he finds that he must be responsive to human need by which he is surrounded, particularly the kind of human need in which the sufferers are victims of circumstances over which, as individuals, they have no control" (Thurman, *Deep Is the Hunger*, 44).
60. Thurman, *Jesus and the Disinherited*, 90.
61. Thurman, *Jesus and the Disinherited*, 90.
62. Thurman, *Jesus and the Disinherited*, 89.
63. Thurman, *Jesus and the Disinherited*, 89.

household of Israel who became his enemies" and loving "those beyond the household of Israel," including the Samaritan and the Roman.[64]

To misunderstand or misrepresent the crucial presence of the Samaritan in Jesus's imaginative tale—as many Good Samaritan Laws do—is to misrepresent the original. (Many critique Augustine for this omission as well, although we cannot claim ignorance on his part.)[65] For Thurman, this "enemy" character is key. Thurman's orientation leads him to discuss a psychological dimension that may not be available to us from the Gospel sources. Attempting to think historically, he defines the enemy within Jesus's context using three categories:

1. A "personal enemy": an individual offense from someone within one's primary group[66]
2. A "second kind of enemy": those whose actions "make it difficult for the group to live without shame and humiliation" (e.g., the tax collector, who "had no soul")[67]
3. A "third type": Rome[68]

The Gospel tradition regularly associates those who collect taxes with sinners (Mark 2:16–17). The latter term, "sinners," implies explicit breaking of Torah. Being associated with this group could place one outside the significant circles of influence within village life in the first century.[69] More crucial for our purposes, Thurman classifies the Samaritans within the third type. From the perspective of Jesus, his

64. Thurman, *Jesus and the Disinherited*, 90.

65. See Patrick Clark's defense of Augustine on this point (above). Also see Fredriksen, *Augustine and the Jews*.

66. Thurman, *Jesus and the Disinherited*, 91–92. Collectivist societies—as was first-century Judaism—may not have exemplified the "personal" offense in this stark way.

67. Thurman, *Jesus and the Disinherited*, 93.

68. Thurman, *Jesus and the Disinherited*, 95–96.

69. See Carey, *Sinners*; Powery, "Tax Collector."

family, and his Jewish friends, Samaritans and Romans were in the same group, even if Rome would have had more political power and thereby would have been potentially more dangerous to their well-being. For Thurman, recognizing the category in which the Samaritans fell may explain the disciples' desire to torch a Samaritan village for its refusal to receive the Jesus group (Luke 9:51–55).

Thurman also considered a second story pivotal for Jesus's understanding of the "enemy" and thereby what Jesus might have meant about the "neighbor." Thurman used his own imaginative gifts when he linked the Luke 10 story to another one of Jesus's encounters in which a non-Jew played a significant role, the story of the Syrophoenician woman in Mark 7 and Matthew 15.[70] Jesus's conversation with her is informative, though not quite in the way that the Gospel narratives reveal. In Thurman's imagination, Jesus was processing the ethnic tension between them by thinking these thoughts to himself: "What right has this woman of another race to make a claim upon me? What mockery is there here? Am I not humiliated enough in being misunderstood by my own kind? And here this woman dares to demand that which, in the very nature of this case, she cannot claim as her due."[71] Thurman's Jesus—like Thurman, who was at the time copastoring an interracial and interfaith congregation in a segregated society—frequently reflected on the ethnological situations of his surroundings.

For Thurman, the manner in which Jesus managed the ethnic conflicts of his day provided a "technique of survival for the oppressed" that could be utilized by any age, including his own as an African American living in the middle decades of twentieth-century US society. Thurman published *Jesus and the Disinherited* five years before *Brown v. Board of Education* (1954). The usefulness of the Samaritan parable was that it revealed Jesus's reflection on the tension between people groups, a reflection in which Jesus had to work

---

70. The story has no parallel in Luke's Gospel.
71. Thurman, *Jesus and the Disinherited*, 91.

out his view of the "neighbor" by thinking through his relationship to the non-Jews around him. The parable was not fundamentally a story about the grand narrative of salvation (per Augustine). For Thurman, the traditional view of salvation—that it alone would be sufficient to excise the ethnic tensions within American society—was insufficient, especially for those outside the power structures of the day: "I do not ignore the theological and metaphysical interpretation of the Christian doctrine of salvation. But the underprivileged everywhere have long since abandoned any hope that this type of salvation deals with the crucial issues by which their days are turned into despair without consolation. The basic fact is that Christianity as it was born in the mind of this Jewish teacher and thinker appears as a technique of survival for the oppressed."[72] Thurman was already thinking this way years before the writing of *Jesus and the Disinherited*. As a copastor of an interfaith church, he promoted incessantly the religion *of* Jesus rather than the religion *about* Jesus. Gary Dorrien's assessment may not be too far off the mark: "Thurman had little interest in formal theology and no interest at all in theological orthodoxy."[73]

Within *Jesus and the Disinherited*, Thurman does not provide a detailed summary of the Luke 10 parable. In order to find his retelling of the story, we turn our attention to a sermon he preached a few years after his *Jesus* book appeared, a sermon preached to his congregation in San Francisco.

A 1951 Sermon on the Parable

Many of Thurman's 1950s sermons were working out the thesis he laid bare in *Jesus and the Disinherited* on the usefulness of Jesus's

---

72. Thurman, *Jesus and the Disinherited*, 29. Thurman came to this conclusion early in his theological journey (*With Head and Heart*, 115–17).

73. Dorrien, *Making of American Liberal Theology*, 562. See also Vincent Harding's assessment: "Thurman had developed an approach to (or better, a relationship with) Jesus of Nazareth that took him beyond the central orthodoxy of American Christianity" (foreword to *Jesus and the Disinherited*, v).

teaching, actions, and life for the dispossessed of every age, including African Americans living in segregated America. Thurman's sermon on the good Samaritan story, which was preached on October 7, 1951, provided a fuller explanation of how Thurman understood the role of the Samaritan in Jesus's thinking and the implications of this story for his own theological reflection and humanizing work.

In a series of thematic sermons preached on passages from Luke's Gospel, Thurman provided his own retelling of Jesus's "simple story," with some informative internal commentary along the way:

> That a certain man went along a certain road. It was a very dangerous road, from Jerusalem down to Jericho. And he fell among thieves, and thieves did to him what thieves would do. They took what he had, and he didn't like it so much. He resisted, apparently, so they injured him, and left him stripped of his goods, and also sick, wounded. And along the way came a priest who did not take any cognizance of his presence or condition. The great phrase is that he walked by on the other side; much has been done with that. It's a nice phrase. And then another man came along, [a man] who was, in a sense, a kind of assistant to the priest, who represented also a whole hierarchy of cultural influences of his own and he walked by without paying any attention to the destitute man by the roadside. And then a third man came by who was a Samaritan. A Samaritan was a man who, in the minds of many of the people who were listening to the story that Jesus told, . . . lived on the other side of the tracks. He was almost there but wasn't quite there. So this Samaritan ministered to the needs of this helpless man by pouring oil and wine on his wounds, cleaning him up, and then he put him on his donkey and carried him to a little resting place, an inn, that evidently was protected, and he said to the innkeeper, "Now take care of this man, and any expenses beyond the money that I am giving you now that are involved, I will repay you when I return." And Jesus said that the man who befriended the destitute individual was the man who showed the neighborly attitude.[74]

74. Thurman, "Good Samaritan," 49.

Those familiar with the general direction of the story will find little new information here. Those who remember details of the KJV's translation of the story—the Bible Thurman would have read[75]—may discover subtle differences, which seem key for understanding Thurman's approach to the parable. To be sure, before he examines the parable with "two or three observations," he provides his initial general assessment of the story: "Who is my neighbor, according to the story? Any [person][76] whose need calls me, and I respond to that need?"[77]

But Thurman's interpretation of what he calls a "simple story" moves beyond this modest conclusion.[78] In fact, Thurman challenges the idea that mercy should respond only to need, since human need never ends![79]

For Thurman, then, the basis of the story is that "Jesus seems to be insisting that we relate ourselves to the person."[80] In that vein, without explicitly acknowledging it, Thurman redefines the details of the story to make a fuller point: we must "relate ourselves to the person." To put it another way, Thurman's reiteration of the story, with its many subtle revisions, humanizes the characters of the story. For example,

> Thurman gives agency to the unnamed victim: "He didn't like it so much. He resisted, apparently, so they injured him." The victim became a more prominent *subject* in Thurman's retelling.[81]
>
> The thieves intended only to commit the theft until the man resisted; then they hurt him. Thurman's implication is that it was not their intention to wound him from the beginning.

75. Thurman was interested in more recent translations as well (*With Head and Heart*, 66–67), but the dependence on the KJV is evident whenever he opened a sermon with a reading of the passage.

76. I utilize inclusive language here in the spirit of Thurman's own desire for more humanizing language.

77. Thurman, "Good Samaritan," 51.

78. Thurman, "Good Samaritan," 49.

79. Thurman, "Good Samaritan," 54–55.

80. Thurman, "Good Samaritan," 54.

81. In the Greek text of Luke 10:30, the "victim" was the subject of (only) two actions: he "went down" the road and "fell" into the hands of robbers.

The priest in Thurman's account did not really notice the victim; he "did not take any cognizance of his presence or condition." It may still imply that he saw him, but he did not *really* see him—so the priest was not to be blamed in the way he is often depicted in many later interpretations.

The "assistant to the priest" also walked by "without paying any attention" to the man on the roadside; again, he is described similarly as the priest.

Outside of the parable proper, even the lawyer receives Thurman's humanizing effect since Thurman omits the lawyer's "test" (Luke 10:25) and, more importantly, omits that the lawyer "wanted to justify himself" (10:29). Despite Luke's characteristics, Thurman depicts him as sincere.[82]

On Thurman's lips, this is a story in which no character is depicted with ill intentions. Each one is described as sincere, even if some are sincerely misguided. How one tells a story matters. Language matters. Spoken words may (intentionally or not) include or exclude some listeners. For Thurman, even retelling biblical stories required acts of humanization.[83] This was especially true in the context of Thurman's multiracial and interfaith congregation. Thurman offered little negative assessment of the Jewish practices of the priest or the Levite or what they may represent. After all, Thurman's Jesus was one firmly planted within first-century Jewish life: "The miracle of the Jewish people is almost as breathtaking as the miracle of Jesus."[84]

One week earlier, in a sermon on forgiveness, Thurman offered the following remark on the Gospels' "judgmental attitude" toward the

---

82. More surprising perhaps, Thurman's lawyer did *not* provide the final answer to his initial question as in Luke's account. Instead, Jesus supplied the punch line: "Jesus said that the man who befriended the destitute individual was the man who showed the neighborly attitude" ("Good Samaritan," 51).

83. The general tenor of the story remains, but the nuances are noticeable.

84. Thurman, *Jesus and the Disinherited*, 15.

Pharisees, an observation common among biblical scholars today but much less so in the US society of the mid-twentieth century: "Most of the New Testament references to the Pharisees are references that reflect a judgmental attitude toward the Pharisee that [does not acknowledge] . . . the genius of the Pharisaic movement in Israel. It is a reflection of another kind of attitude, [a] kind of prejudice, and this of course is nothing new, nothing radical; it's an old familiar thing to those persons who have made any study of either the Pharisees or the Sadducees or of Israel or of the life of Jesus for that matter."[85] Though less explicit, the same attitude can be found in Thurman's slight adjustments to the Samaritan story.

For the contemporary Thurman, one of the challenges of the story is in the personal interaction between two individuals: "It's much [easier] to forgive a national enemy . . . than it is to forgive a personal enemy," because "there [are] going into the matrix of your relatedness all of the rich overtones of your private living and desiring and fellowship," and "you must forgive at every point of your relatedness."[86] This is the true meaning of love: "I'm involved in an encounter that leads from the core of me to the core of you."[87]

As Jesus humanized the "other" by giving the Samaritan the active hero role in his story, so Thurman humanized the other by deemphasizing the qualities that may have forced us to think negatively of the priest's or the Levite's or the lawyer's actions. One should assume the humanity of the other in order to maintain one's own integrity and sense of worth.

At the end of the sermon, Thurman summons his congregants to the challenge: "What about it?" Moreover, Thurman imagines a world of the possible: "To that degree it is a reasonable thing to dream about a time when this world will be a decent place for friendly

85. Thurman, "Forgiveness," 40. Later in his autobiography, Thurman discusses the influence on his thinking of Louis Finkelstein's 1938 classic, *The Pharisees*. See Thurman, *With Head and Heart*, 149.

86. Thurman, "Good Samaritan," 55.

87. Thurman, "Good Samaritan," 55.

[people] underneath a friendly sky. Let's try it and see."[88] Jesus's parable about an imaginary human interaction in an imaginary world became paramount for the way Thurman's dream took shape, even if he was attempting to update the Gospel story in light of the "religion of Jesus." As Luther Smith, Thurman's biographer, acknowledges, "Thurman's preaching insists that we are living the parables" in the here and now.[89]

Jesus and the Disinherited, *King, and the Samaritan*

The impact of Thurman's teaching and life was (and continues to be) far-reaching. Apparently, Martin Luther King Jr. carried Thurman's *Jesus and the Disinherited* in his briefcase along with the parables (i.e., his Bible).[90] If true, then how King interpreted Jesus and the stories of Jesus may have been shaped by the great mystic prophet. According to Gary Dorrien, this dependence is explicit: King's "sermons drew on Thurman's insights. Progressive American Christianity has no greater legacy than that."[91]

King also loved to preach on the Samaritan story. It shows up many times in his sermons and speeches. Most significantly for our purposes is how King utilized his own creative energies to move beyond the parable proper in order to remember the moral necessity of Jesus's story. Even King's public speeches offer theological critique through biblical imagery, like the one from 1967 in which he challenged the US involvement in the Vietnam War: "We are called to play the Good Samaritan on life's roadside; but that will be only an initial act. One day the whole Jericho Road must be transformed so that men and women will not be beaten and robbed as they make their journey through life. True compassion is more than flinging a coin

88. Thurman, "Good Samaritan," 56.
89. Smith, foreword to *Sermons on the Parables*, xiii.
90. Thurman credits Lerone Bennett's book *What Manner of Man* for making the observation that King carried *Jesus and the Disinherited* "in his briefcase." See Thurman, *With Head and Heart*, 255.
91. Dorrien, *Making of American Liberal Theology*, 566.

to a beggar; it understands that an edifice which produces beggars needs restructuring."[92] Giving to those in need is not unimportant, but King takes his audience in a radically different direction when he thinks seriously about what Thurman referred to as the "dangerous" road down to Jericho. In light of the American context dealing with the crises of—in King's words—rising militarism, ongoing racism, and degrading poverty, King imagined the possibility that the "road to Jericho" would be completely transformed so that the tragedies happening on that road would no longer occur. King imagined a world order that would deal with the "Jerichos" of today. Though Thurman outlived King, King's view of Jesus may have been crucially dependent on Thurman's *Jesus and the Disinherited*.[93]

Summary

For Thurman, the usefulness of the parable was to view Jesus's story as one about tensions between people groups and as one in which Jesus himself attempted to imagine a human relationship different from what he and others experienced. Thurman explained that Jesus developed his view of neighbor by thinking through his experience among non-Jewish people in his context. This "fact" had implications for Thurman's use of the Samaritan story.

For Thurman's Jesus the personal encounter mattered, so that individuals must become willing to commit to a life of peaceful interactions with a variety of people in a variety of contexts. Crucial to this perspective was Thurman's ability to retell stories from the biblical tradition. As mentioned earlier, how one tells a story matters! Language matters. For Thurman, this meant that the way one passed along the stories of the faith also required (linguistic) acts of humanization.

92. King, *Where Do We Go from Here*, 198.
93. Fluker and Tumber highlight the impact *Jesus and the Disinherited* had elsewhere: both "Gandhian ideas" and Thurman's work at the Fellowship Church "received a larger audience through the publication of his most famous book, *Jesus and the Disinherited*," which also deeply influenced leaders of the civil rights struggle in the 1950s (Fluker and Tumber, *Strange Freedom*, 6).

The Luke 10 Parable and the Solentiname Community

> Our vision and God's become one, as if God were in our eyes.
>
> Ernesto Cardenal, *Abide in Love*

> Poverty is . . . closest to our true condition, while riches are a disguise.
>
> Ernesto Cardenal, *Abide in Love*

An Introduction to Solentiname and Its Communal Project

The Solentiname community in Nicaragua produced a vibrant and accessible collection of popular communal Bible studies in the 1970s. Ernesto Cardenal, a poet and priest, served as minister for ninety families—approximately one thousand people who lived on the largest segments of the thirty-eight islands in the archipelago of Solentiname.[94] Even with all of these families, few attended Mass. Cardenal explains why: "Many because they had no boat, and others because they missed the devotion to the saints, to which they were accustomed. Others stayed away through the influence of anti-Communist propaganda, and perhaps also through fear."[95] Partly due to these obstacles, Cardenal, along with others, formed a "contemplative community" engaged in poetry writing and art, in addition to regular Bible discussions.[96] Those who were unhindered physically, spiritually, or politically and gathered for these conversations became part of recorded history.

The "commentary" project that grew out of these discussions took on a life of its own. Following Mass, in lieu of a sermon, the group would have what Cardenal called a "dialogue," a discussion in which the group thought with Scripture.[97] The richness of the conversations encouraged Cardenal to capture these dialogues for posterity.

94. Cardenal, *Gospel in Solentiname*, 3:viii.
95. Cardenal, *Gospel in Solentiname*, 3:ix.
96. Two other poets—William Agudelo and Carlos Alberto—assisted in the founding of the community in 1966, partially inspired by Thomas Merton. See Gullette, *Nicaraguan Peasant Poetry*, 5; Reed, "Bible, Religious Storytelling, and Revolution," 236; Gowler, *Parables after Jesus*, 233.
97. Cardenal, *Gospel in Solentiname*, 3:vii.

Many of these Bible studies occurred over meals. This is evident in some of the discussions, as in the one on Luke 10:38–42, a story in which Mary and Martha have chosen separate activities but Jesus affirms Mary's action as "the better part." The Nicaraguan community was debating the passage when Olivia—who was preparing the communal meal for that day—announced that their supper was ready "right now." She additionally confessed, "Food shouldn't prevent us from being interested in the kingdom."[98]

Since some members of the community could not read, the format of the Bible study was as follows: "Each Sunday we first would distribute copies of the Gospels to those who could read." The passage was read aloud for all. "Then we discussed it verse by verse."[99] In this format Cardenal directed the discussion.[100] For good or for ill, the verse-by-verse format guides a discussion in a particular kind of way, rather than allowing participants to follow whatever direction they deem most significant. This does not necessarily hinder the creative activity of the endeavor.

For Cardenal, their liberationist perspective was consistent with their Bible since the Gospel was written for the poor—that is, for the people of Solentiname—and, equally important, was written "by people like them."[101] Along these lines, in another meditation, Cardenal found poverty to be central to his own view of the Godhead: "Poverty is also a virtue of the Trinity because God's life is communitarian and communistic and each of the three persons gives himself

98. Cardenal, *Gospel in Solentiname*, 3:109. Throughout the exercise the written recording utilizes only first names for most of the contributors. Olivia's comment here should not detract from her theological sophistication in many of these studies (as Cardenal himself recognizes). For example, reflecting on the Mary/Martha story, Olivia says that Martha was "thinking about Christ, without thinking about all of the Christs of today" (Cardenal, *Gospel of Solentiname*, 3:108).

99. Cardenal, *Gospel of Solentiname*, 3:vii–viii.

100. For Reed, Cardenal's engagement added authenticity to the recorded account. See his "Bible, Religious Storytelling, and Revolution," 232.

101. Cardenal, *Gospel of Solentiname*, 3:vii. According to Reed, "The bible studies in Solentiname shifted toward the political, following Cardenal's visit to Cuba in 1970, where he met 'radical Christians' from other Latin American countries" ("Bible, Religious Storytelling, and Revolution," 235).

totally to the others."[102] The observations, then, of this economically poor community would appear to be more in tune with what the ancient authors may have been saying. Generally, the community conflated the contexts. Nevertheless, they occasionally recognized the distance between the two distinct settings—the first-century one and their twentieth-century one. Equally important was how religious storytelling, as Jean-Pierre Reed's analysis recognizes, allowed participants to map their political landscape and thereby their social locations in relationship to the larger political context and world.[103] The communal Bible study encouraged them to interpret their present political climate and locate their physical place within it. Bible study itself becomes a radical exercise.[104] For example, regarding the Mary and Martha story, which on the surface may lend itself less explicitly to a liberationist interpretation, William discovers a political interpretation of the story nonetheless: "Couldn't we sum it up this way: one was a revolutionary and the other wasn't?"[105] As Reed concludes, "a growing number of Nicaraguan Christians" in this context "used the Bible to find justification for the defense of their human dignity."[106]

Finally, despite the involvement of so many contributors, all living in the same tension-filled political context though not all in agreement about the various strategies for how to live as a community in light of their faith (or for some, little religious faith), Cardenal recognized the Spirit's guidance through the practice of Bible study. In the introduction to *The Gospel in Solentiname*, Cardenal credits various individuals involved in the project to acknowledge their roles (and not himself) as the "authors" before he pauses and corrects himself: "I am wrong. The true author is the Spirit that has inspired these commentaries (the Solentiname *campesinos* know very well

102. Cardenal, *Abide in Love*, 95–96.
103. Reed, "Bible, Religious Storytelling, and Revolution," 230.
104. This is the language of Reed: "Bible study discussions made it possible for many Christians in Nicaragua—in and outside Solentiname—to mobilize as revolutionaries" ("Bible, Religious Storytelling, and Revolution," 228).
105. Cardenal, *Gospel of Solentiname*, 3:111.
106. Reed, "Bible, Religious Storytelling, and Revolution," 234–35.

that it is the Spirit who makes them speak) and that it was the Spirit who inspired the Gospels."[107]

The Good Samaritan and the Solentiname Community

For the purposes of this discussion, I want to reflect on the Solentiname community's Bible study on the good Samaritan story in three distinct categories, each of which overlaps with other sections. First, we will examine how they contextualized the biblical story. Second, we will focus on their insights on the parable proper. Finally, we will briefly review their conclusions, which in a communal project of this sort may not necessarily represent all the participants in the conversation. As David Gowler notes, the parables came alive in the community's context and lives: "Their earthy and apparently simple responses often contain profound expressions of their conviction that Jesus and his parables are alive, present with them, and actively working with them and through them."[108]

When interpreting a biblical passage, it is much easier to see how a person from another cultural context is attempting to apply the world of Scripture than to recognize one's own cultural influences. In light of the teacher of the law's question in Luke 10, Alejandro replies, "What was happening then with the law is happening now with the Gospel."[109] Jesus's question to the lawyer, "What do you read there?" (10:26 NRSV), captures this Nicaraguan group's attention. Cardenal continues Alejandro's direction: "It's as if a supporter of this regime should ask us what we think of the Gospels. That could be a dangerous question, couldn't it?"[110] The "danger" of their biblical interpretation may be found throughout this recorded Bible study.

107. Cardenal, *Gospel of Solentiname*, 3:ix. *Campesinos* is the Spanish term for "poor farmers."
108. Gowler, *Parables after Jesus*, 234.
109. Cardenal, *Gospel of Solentiname*, 3:94. The Bible study is published in the format of a written dialogue. In addition to their recorded names, I will use Cardenal whenever the priest speaks; in the dialogue he is listed as "I."
110. Cardenal, *Gospel of Solentiname*, 3:95.

As Cardenal reflects on these communal gatherings years later, "The Gospel made us political revolutionaries."[111] Just to give one example up front, Laureano wishes to update the language for "neighbor" and equate it with the contemporary image of the "comrade." For Laureano and the others, a comrade is a person who holds the same political views as others who suffer under an abusive government.[112] (In the strained political context of North American life in 2020, many of us may resonate with this definition of "comrade.") "Ultimately," as Reed observes, "subversive storytelling shapes the dynamics of social change as it provides identity, solidarity, orientation, and vigor to political actors."[113]

Because of their desire to develop the relevancy of the biblical story for their immediate context, these Latin American interpreters occasionally provided alternative suggestions to the story line. For example, instead of Jesus's initial response to the lawyer ("What does Torah say? How do you read it?"), Laureano remarks that what would have been "dangerous" was if Jesus had said, "Take from the rich what they have and distribute it among the poor."[114] (Laureano may have been unaware that Jesus said similar words to another inquisitor in Luke's Gospel [18:22].) The economic sentiment exemplifies his liberationist preference for the poor, but it also speaks to the immediate contemporary tension between the poor (campesinos) and the rich (landowners), which will reappear throughout the discussion.

How does their reading of Jesus's story of the Samaritan offer insight into these contemporary economic disparities? The Solentiname community, this "lay monastery" community, as Cardenal refers to them, attempts to unpack the biblical story for their context.[115]

---

111. Cf. Gullette, *Nicaraguan Peasant Poetry*, 11.
112. Cardenal, *Gospel of Solentiname*, 3:99. It is unclear whether Laureano or Cardenal draws this conclusion initially within this segment. What is clear is that both agree in the end.
113. Reed, "Bible, Religious Storytelling, and Revolution," 230.
114. Cardenal, *Gospel of Solentiname*, 3:95.
115. Cardenal, *Gospel of Solentiname*, 3:viii.

Similar to their North American counterparts, the Solentiname people express a strong bias against the lawyer (and priest and Levite). For example, regarding the lawyer's response to Jesus (to love God and love neighbor), Laureano says, "Jesus makes him say things he doesn't do." Laureano assumes the insincerity of the lawyer, which may be tapping into Luke's description of the lawyer as one who was seeking "to justify himself" (10:29). But Laureano did not provide any specific Lukan support for his assessment.

Other contributors move beyond the Lukan text altogether. An unnamed person (simply called "Another" within the recorded collection) suggests that the lawyer may have wanted to argue about "other laws that were nonsense" and gives specific examples such as "worship in the temple, the Sabbath, unclean food, purification."[116] Alejandro suggests that the lawyer "realizes that he had never loved his neighbor"; he loved God, "but neighbor, shit, up to then he didn't even know who he was."[117] Olivia picks up this thread but spins it around: the lawyer "didn't know his neighbor because he didn't have love." A few comments later she says, "Your neighbors are all of humanity."[118] This revolutionary spirit, which is evident in this gathering, is often quite interested in love—that is, who has it, how it is defined, and to whom it is given. Finally, Rebeca at least gives the lawyer credit for what she calls a "selfish love"—that is, love for his own children and his close friends, just not for others outside his family circle.[119]

North American academic critiques of liberation theological interpreters' tendencies suggest that liberationists often provide anti-Semitic readings.[120] To be fair, this inclination is not exclusive to lib-

---

116. Cardenal, *Gospel of Solentiname*, 3:95.
117. Cardenal, *Gospel of Solentiname*, 3:96.
118. Cardenal, *Gospel of Solentiname*, 3:96.
119. Cardenal, *Gospel of Solentiname*, 3:96.
120. See Levine, "Disease of Postcolonial New Testament Studies," 91–99. This article was part of the "Roundtable Discussion: Anti-Judaism and Postcolonial Biblical Interpretation." Respondents included Kwok Pui-lan, Musimbi Kanyoro, Adele Reinhartz, Hisako Kinukawa, and Elaine Wainwright.

eration exegetes; many North American Christian interpreters draw similar conclusions on Jewish characters who challenge Jesus in the Gospels.[121] Cardenal's Bible study gathering was not Howard Thurman's interfaith community. The interpretation itself, however, is not surprising because the Solentiname readers were thinking much more about their own contemporary enemies than about the "historical" characters and caricatures of the Gospel of Luke.

------------------------ ■ ------------------------

Regarding the parable proper, Olivia initiates this part of the discussion, depicting the Samaritan character as "a person of another race and another religion" and acknowledging that Jesus's extreme choice of the "enemy" as a "neighbor" was so that "we can know that everybody is a neighbor."[122] Jesus's imaginative choice in the parable is inclusive of everybody, not an individual representative of an exclusive party. But Manuel strips the Samaritan of any religious label altogether, comparing him to the other two characters in the parable. He discovers a significant difference between the religious ones and the character he calls the "heretic": "Some take care of the temple but not of neighbors, and so they are evil, and the other one didn't take care of the temple; he was a heretic, and he was the good one."[123] Along these lines, "Another" (unnamed) agrees with Manuel, acknowledging what we can find in many contemporary North American commentaries on the story: "It was religion itself that prevented them from loving their neighbor, and that kind of thing is still going on."[124]

While some will criticize this liberationist community for what seems like an anti-Judaism conclusion, Olivia reminds us that these

121. J. Sanders, *Jews in Luke-Acts*, 183.
122. Cardenal, *Gospel of Solentiname*, 3:97. For Luke's view of the Samaritan and the Samaritan community, see chap. 3.
123. Cardenal, *Gospel of Solentiname*, 3:97.
124. Cardenal, *Gospel of Solentiname*, 3:98.

labels (e.g., the person's religion) reveal much more about the contemporary context than the ancient one: "It's hard to be a Christian, like the Samaritan was. It's easier to be just religious, like so many Catholics are, and be praying to God in the temple."[125] It is not the temples of old that trouble this Latin American community but the present ones that support abusive governmental regimes and shore up the side of oppressors or that, in a posture of neutrality, offer their complicity by their silence. For this Nicaraguan community, reading the Bible was a spiritual practice; reading the Bible was also a political practice. The two—the spiritual and the political—could not be easily separated.

Despite Olivia's initial reaction to the Samaritan's distinct religious leanings, which is probably closer to the historical reality of the first century, others in the Bible study prefer an a-religious description of the man: "The man without religion was the neighbor."[126] More than likely, the ancient Samaritan in Jesus's story had his own religious views and also had a sacred text (the Pentateuch) that stipulated care for the dispossessed.

Moving in a different direction, Laureano wishes to update the language of "neighbor" to "comrade" (as mentioned earlier) since it is not easy to discern what "neighborly love" might mean in the present.[127] After Cardenal chimes in, seeking clarification, Laureano continues, "Love of your neighbor is comradeship." It was not simply giving the man material goods directly. "He took him to a hotel and paid for his room" and promised to pay extra later, so "of course, from then on they remained friends; they were already comrades."[128] For Laureano, the parable becomes an allegory of his own setting: distinct from the "religious people" who disregard people's problems, "the atheists who are revolutionaries are the good Samaritan of the

125. Cardenal, *Gospel of Solentiname*, 3:103.
126. Cardenal, *Gospel of Solentiname*, 3:98. Even Cardenal, who knew better, refers to him as a "pagan" later in the discussion (3:100).
127. Cardenal, *Gospel of Solentiname*, 3:98.
128. Cardenal, *Gospel of Solentiname*, 3:98–99.

parable, the good companion, the good comrade."[129] At times, false dichotomies would arise in the discussion. Could this Samaritan not have cared for the human dignity of others—like a true comrade, a Communist could—and still have loved his God? Was not Cardenal both a priest and a Communist supporter?

Unsurprisingly, at this point in the dialogue there was a bias against the priest and the Levite, as well as against the lawyer earlier, moving beyond Jesus's specified intentions. Someone noticed—perhaps due to the "religious" practice of Bible study they were engaged in—that the condemnation of all religious people is an improper generalization. Cardenal, after all, was moderating the discussion. So a minor debate occurred about whether the religious characters—the priest and the Levite—should not also be included in the concept of neighbors. How insightful it was! Eventually, an unnamed man from San Miguelito responds (it seems with some passion, since the transcription says he "insisted"), "Neighbors are the whole human race."[130] Within the group, not all agreed. Manuel would not let him have the last word: "Jesus makes it clear that some, because they're selfish, stop being neighbors of others."[131] Can individuals take themselves out of the communal neighborhood by selfish acts?

Interpreting this parable in the immediacy of their tension-filled political context, this group found immediate connections between love for God and love for neighbor. With respect to the lawyer, their comments emphatically focused on distinctions between two types of love. The lawyer failed, from their perspective, to understand how the two were directly linked. According to Elvis, speaking for the first time in reaction to the absence of loving God, "It's that those who love their neighbor are right there loving God."[132] Cardenal affirms this assessment, after pointing to several other biblical passages in which love of neighbor is elevated, so that "in this parable he [Jesus]

129. Cardenal, *Gospel of Solentiname*, 3:99.
130. Cardenal, *Gospel of Solentiname*, 3:100.
131. Cardenal, *Gospel of Solentiname*, 3:100.
132. Cardenal, *Gospel of Solentiname*, 3:101.

shows that the two [love commands] are fulfilled by fulfilling the second [commandment]."[133] Earlier, Cardenal had offered a similar reaction to Manuel's distinction between the "religious" and the "heretic": "Those who love God without loving their neighbor are not carrying out the law, but they are carrying out the law if they love their neighbor without loving God."[134]

This led to an interesting repartee between Cardenal ("I," below) and Laureano, apparently the most politically radical member of the group, about the existence of God.[135] If Jesus is saying that acting kindly or loving one's neighbor is the same as loving God, then what might Jesus's words imply about God?

> Laureano: "He's saying that there's no God, then, that God is your neighbor."
>
> I: "He's saying that God is love."
>
> Laureano: "He's saying that to love others, that's God."
>
> I: "He's saying that there is a God, but God is that."
>
> Laureano: "God is all of us then."
>
> I: "Love. All, but united; not all separated, hating each other or exploiting each other."[136]

So God is present when love is present. Moreover, God is present when the community is present. At the end of this jousting scene, Cardenal conjures Augustine: "Saint Augustine says God is the love with which we love each other."[137] The significance of this mini-debate within the larger dialogue is not lost on the other participants. Right after Augustine is cited, Alejandro exclaims, "What has been said here

---

133. Cardenal, *Gospel of Solentiname*, 3:102.

134. Cardenal, *Gospel of Solentiname*, 3:97.

135. In his introduction to the collection, Cardenal describes Laureano as the one "who refers everything to the Revolution" (Cardenal, *Gospel of Solentiname*, 3:ix). Several participants in this dialogue eventually participated militarily in the revolution.

136. Cardenal, *Gospel of Solentiname*, 3:102.

137. Cardenal, *Gospel of Solentiname*, 3:103.

is very important!"[138] Most of us would agree with Alejandro, Augustine, and Cardenal.[139] In fact, it is difficult to distinguish Cardenal, Thurman, and Augustine on the topic of love: "God is love. And is there any greater joy than to love and be loved? God is God because God is love, because he is the joy of love. God is the infinite joy of infinite love."[140]

Even without fully understanding the immediate context, readers should be able to grasp the political dimensions of their interpretation. This spiritual, communal practice was intimately linked with civic engagement, especially an engagement that beckoned the group to stand with those unable to speak for themselves. Reading the gospel turned them toward the political, as Cardenal would put it elsewhere. Although some interpreters may have overlooked this direction throughout the dialogue, the political becomes even more explicit in the ending of the discussion.

First, "Another" calls out the government-sponsored sermons, indirectly calling into question the traditional view of salvation (in a manner similar to that of Thurman): "That gringo preacher, Spencer, who preaches everyday sweetly about the spiritual salvation of Christ, he's probably a CIA agent."[141] This statement condemns the US government's support of the oppressive regime in Nicaragua. Clearly, the traditional "spiritual salvation" is distinct from the message of salvation they themselves discovered and promoted in their Bible interrogations. There is salvation here for them as well, but it is one

138. Cardenal, *Gospel of Solentiname*, 3:103.

139. Another interesting allegorical move near the end is Cardenal's drawing the Samaritan woman (John 4) into this story in order to utilize Jesus's idea that "now God wasn't going to be adorned in temples but everywhere 'in spirit and in truth.' Since then we Christians have filled the earth with temples, but Jesus taught us that the only temple is the human being. The man fallen by the wayside in Jerusalem, he was the temple" (Cardenal, *Gospel of Solentiname*, 3:103; cf. 1 Cor. 6:19). But this seems more like an academic exegetical move on Cardenal's part, not indicative of the popular reading practices of the group.

140. Cardenal, *Abide in Love*, 32.

141. Cardenal, *Gospel of Solentiname*, 3:104. This critique mimics Thurman's emphasis on the inadequacy of the traditional teaching of salvation to assist the marginalized.

that encourages them to lean toward one another in an engagement with liberating, saving, and sustaining practices on earth.

Second, an unnamed "South American Hippie," as he is described, recognizes that enemies, too, are neighbors; nonetheless, these enemies have been deceived.[142] Consequently, he advises others to love them too and convince them of the truth. Jesus's story encouraged him to recognize the necessity of love even for those relationships defined by opposition. He admits that there are other elements of the story that the group has left untouched; for example, he suggests that the assailants point allegorically to "the exploiters who have legally assaulted the people, with the laws that they themselves have made."[143] Again, their allegorical interpretive moves—even if they weren't part of a formal reading practice, as they were in Augustine's day—could bring meaning to other elements of the story.

Finally, at the end of this explicit stretch toward the political, Laureano contributes again. In this recording of the Bible study on the good Samaritan story, he has the last word and final reinterpretation of the account, which, in turn, may sum up well the thinking of many members of the group: "And while religion went along that road without looking at the wounded man, communism, which didn't believe in God, has been the good companion that took up the wounded man and took him to a shelter where he could have food and a roof and clothing and medicine, *all free*."[144] The good Samaritan is the good, generous, financially and emotionally supportive comrade, known in their time frame and context as the good revolutionary Communist.[145]

---

142. This contributor also affirms something Laureano says, which shows the kind of support and influence Laureano had on the group. Cardenal, *Gospel of Solentiname*, 3:104.

143. Cardenal, *Gospel of Solentiname*, 3:104.

144. Cardenal, *Gospel of Solentiname*, 3:104 (my italics).

145. Reed links the format of the Bible study to the nature of the formation of radical ideas: "Its open-ended and informal nature . . . also makes it possible for story-users to communicate *more* effectively across social differences and to explore varied dimensions of their identities and correspondingly to come together based on a common interest, idea, or goal" ("Bible, Religious Storytelling, and Revolution," 229).

Summary

What do we learn from this communal practice about interpreting the good Samaritan story? Many questions remain. The conclusion of the Bible study—like a good Toni Morrison novel—is open ended. Did they all agree with Laureano's final thoughts? Did they all assume that religion, broadly speaking, and their Catholic faith (even with Cardenal living among them) supported more consistently the status quo? Moreover, this should raise a question for us: Why do many North American Bible studies, theological dialogues, or Sunday sermons ignore the political situation in which we find ourselves?

These Bible studies were not quite subversive storytelling practices in and of themselves—unlike, perhaps, the poetry sessions of the Solentiname community—but they did seem to allow for revolutionary interpretations within an immediate context in light of the nature of the subversive parable Jesus told. For this community, reading the Bible was a spiritual practice; however, reading the Bible was also a political practice. Evident in this weekly gathering, the radical spirit is captivated by love—that is, who has love, how it is defined, and to whom it is given. Along with Augustine and Thurman, this Nicaraguan community desired to grapple with the function of love. But love of neighbor is more than a surface expression, because the neighbor is defined as one wholly committed to the other person's well-being, their spiritual *and* social well-being.

One final historical note on Solentiname: under the Somoza government, the San Carlos assault destroyed the "lay monastery" at Solentiname. Several of the participants in this recorded dialogue joined oppositional forces; some of them died. Before this destruction in 1977, Cardenal gathered and published the commentaries.[146] Eventually, after the overthrow of Somoza's government in 1979, many returned to Solentiname. Not long after, those who eventually

---

146. Gowler discusses the dangerous implications of their interpretations, many of which led to some of these actions (*Parables after Jesus*, 235).

returned to the community began to paint, to write poetry, and to rebuild.[147]

Harriet Jacobs and the Enslaved Samaritan

Introduction to Harriet Jacobs's Incidents in the Life of a Slave Girl

Linda Brent is an odd heroine. In a day when female superheroes grace the screens in movie theaters for good reason, it is hard to imagine a woman who hides out in her grandmother's garret for seven years as a heroine capable of inspiring future generations. Then again, context is key, and mid-nineteenth-century antebellum United States is the setting. Linda Brent was an African American woman whose legal status as an enslaved person made her the "property" of another human being. Her hideout was an attempt to escape her master's sight. Why not escape the South altogether? Well, children were involved. At least her grandmother's house—or attic—allowed her a daily opportunity to observe their lives, even if she could not intervene in any direct way without revealing her secret.

Incidents in the Life of a Slave Girl is a much more complicated story than my brief description implies, and it is the story Harriet Jacobs tells about her life in bondage over twenty years prior. "Linda Brent" is her character name. Her narrative is one of dozens of stories written before the American Civil War by formerly enslaved individuals who had escaped the institution of human bondage supported by the politics and laws of this land. Among these stories, Jacobs's is the first one to include on the title page "written by herself"—that is, it is the first one written by a female author herself.[148] According to her biographer, Jean Fagan Yellin, it is also the first one to address an

---

147. Scharper and Scharper, Gospel in Art, 5.
148. Other female narratives had preceded Jacobs's—e.g., Mary Prince's (1831) and Sojourner Truth's (1850)—though they dictated their stories to white editors. For a discussion on the role of agency within these female-dictated narratives in comparison to Jacobs's own, see Santamarina, "Black Womanhood."

explicitly female audience.[149] The title page itself—absent the author's name—carried detailed evidence of this attention to a female audience. A white female editor, Lydia Maria Childs, graced the cover, along with an epigram from "an unnamed woman of North Carolina" that she borrowed from a speech by Angelina Grimké, another famous white abolitionist.[150] Finally, Jacobs apparently marked her title page with the Bible to make her final appeal to women, drawing on words from the prophet Isaiah: "Rise up, ye women that are at ease; hear my voice, ye careless daughters; give ear unto my speech" (Isa. 32:9 KJV).[151]

The "freedom narratives" (or, more popularly, "slave narratives") became one common public source for detailing the daily lives of millions of African Americans held in bondage prior to the American Civil War. From the mid-1840s through the 1850s, these narratives were on the rise, as the Northern public desired to gain more firsthand knowledge about the peculiar institution. Many of these accounts attracted public attention. Jacobs ventured to tell her own story not as a public *speech*—a common practice of the day—but as a series of short stories published in Horace Greeley's popular newspaper, the *New-York Tribune*.[152]

More importantly for our purposes, the Bible plays a central role in the story Jacobs tells in *Incidents*. Many proslavery advocates used the Bible to support arguments in favor of the slave institution, but Jacobs challenged traditional theological views of God, as when she

149. Yellin, "Texts and Contexts," 263.

150. She may have read the following epigram in Angelina Grimké's writings: "Northerners know nothing at all about Slavery. They think it is perpetual bondage only. They have no conception of the depth of *degradation* involved in that word, Slavery; if they had, they would never cease their efforts until so horrible a system was overthrown" (her italics). See Grimké's 1836 essay, "Appeal to the Christian Women of the South," 200. Jacobs's biographer, Jean Fagan Yellin, does not discuss the origins of the title page—whether the author (Jacobs) or the editor (Childs) initiated it—in *Harriet Jacobs: A Life*.

151. For a discussion of the use of Isaiah on the title page of Jacobs's narrative, see Powery and Sadler, *Genesis of Liberation*, 40–45.

152. The first article appeared in 1853. See Yellin, *Harriet Jacobs Family Papers*, 196–200.

heard the news of her father's death: "My heart rebelled against God, who had taken from me mother, father, mistress, and friend."[153] Yet as she found ways to push back against these (theological?) ideas—including the "accommodationist" ones her beloved grandmother espoused[154]—she continued to use the Bible as a resource for justice and social change. Like many formerly enslaved authors, she found justice to be pivotal to the Bible. Moreover, she used it to appeal to the white women of the North.[155]

An Exploration of "The Church and Slavery" in the Nineteenth Century

Other interpreters discussed in this chapter thus far developed their views of the Samaritan parable within ecclesial settings. Luke presents Jesus's parable within a larger narrative about a Jesus who brings "good news to the poor" in a Jewish context that increasingly includes non-Jews. Augustine's sermons and *On Christian Doctrine*, Thurman's sermons and *Jesus and the Disinherited*, and Cardenal's organized Bible studies all presume ecclesial environments. Jacobs's utilization of the Luke 10 parable, however, was situated intentionally within a broader public conversation, although for a biblically literate audience. Her allusion to the parable reveals to readers much about her understanding of the passage and her alternative way of reading.

By the 1850s a number of freedom narratives had received a wide public hearing among Northern abolitionists. *Narrative of the Life of Frederick Douglass, an American Slave* was as popular in that day as it is now. *Uncle Tom's Cabin* (1852) also prepared white audiences for other human bondage stories. Shortly after the publication of *Uncle Tom's Cabin*, Jacobs took up her pen and found her own public voice to support Harriet Beecher Stowe's fictional project:

153. Jacobs, *Incidents*, 18.
154. See Carson, "Dismantling the House of the Lord," 61.
155. For a full introduction to Jacobs's use of the Bible, see Powery, "'Rise Up, Ye Women.'"

"Because one friend of a slave has dared to tell of their wrongs you would annihilate her. But in Uncle Tom's Cabin she has not told the half. Would that I had one spark from her store house of genius and talent I would tell you of my own sufferings."[156] So with her pen Jacobs began to draft the initial pages of *Incidents*, encouraged by her dear friend, Amy Post.

Jacobs's appropriation of Jesus's parable falls within a section called "The Church and Slavery." This exploration became common within narrative traditions as the formerly enslaved attempted to describe their experiences of the ecclesial contexts on Southern plantations.[157] Even though Jacobs occasionally named names, this section offered primarily representative examples of these ecclesial situations, especially in the months immediately following the Nat Turner Revolt.[158] In her community in Edenton, North Carolina, many white citizens thought it necessary after the Turner uprising "to give the slaves enough of religious instruction to keep them from murdering their masters."[159]

Hearing a white minister—in this case, the Reverend Mr. Pike—preach sermons on "Slaves, obey your masters" from the Bible was common.[160] The key to Pike's sermon, as Jacobs records it, was "if you disobey your earthly master, you offend your heavenly Master."[161] Such was the conventional religious experience of many enslaved communities during antebellum days. A theological burden was

156. Jacobs, "Letter from a Fugitive Slave." Jacobs gave her public support to the publication of *Uncle Tom's Cabin* despite Stowe's refusal to transcribe or edit Jacobs's story.

157. Jacobs, *Incidents*, 105–16.

158. Jacobs sets this section on the church and slavery within the context of the immediate aftermath of the 1831 Nat Turner uprising in which at least sixty white people were killed in a twenty-four-hour period; in retaliation, over one hundred black people were killed. See Franklin and Moss, *From Slavery to Freedom*, 164–65.

159. Jacobs, *Incidents*, 105.

160. For a more extensive examination of these "Slaves, obey your masters" sermons—including Pike's sermon—from the freedom narrative tradition, see Powery and Sadler, *Genesis of Liberation*, 113–43.

161. Jacobs, *Incidents*, 107.

invoked to demand the enslaved person's obedience to her slaveholding master. Jacobs relays how poorly these types of sermons were
received by believers of a darker hue. But many would suffer through
these white-led services in order to gain some separate time for their
preferred "Methodist shout": "They never seem so happy as when
shouting and singing at religious meetings."[162] Nevertheless, Jacobs
wanted readers to know that this sort of "shouting" happiness was
limited as well: "If you were to hear them at such times, you might
think they were happy. But can that hour of singing and shouting
sustain them through the dreary week, toiling without wages, under
constant dread of the lash?"[163] Fully aware of the public nature of
this discourse, Jacobs wrote with the clear objective of interven-
ing on behalf of the downtrodden. Yet her complicated narrative
indirectly called into question the sustaining power of both ecclesial
communities, white and black. For her, however, this publication
was not the time to critique all religious gatherings. Some spiritual
practices opposed human dignity and human longing much more
explicitly.

Reflecting further on black spirituality, Jacobs detailed a moving
reflection on the composition of "their own songs"—that is, the songs
of the enslaved—what we would call "spirituals" today.[164] The context
for this narration is one of the most heart-wrenching stories in the
entire freedom-narrative tradition. When visiting a Methodist church
in her youth, Jacobs participated in a testimony service and heard one
woman "testify" that all of her children had been cruelly taken from
her (including her youngest, a daughter who was sixteen): "I've got
nothing to live for now," she testified. "God make my time short!" The
white leader—the "town constable" who "bought and sold slaves"

162. Jacobs, *Incidents*, 107. Jacobs's observation seems to be a subtle critique
of her peers.

163. Jacobs, *Incidents*, 109. Angelina Grimké shared this view of the mythic
"happy slave": "I have never seen a happy slave. I have seen him dance in his chains,
it is true; but he was not happy" (Webb, "Speech of Angelina," 124).

164. Jacobs, *Incidents*, 107–8.

himself—guiding this part of the service did not (could not!) fully grasp the depth of this mother's grief, so other enslaved members broke out with one of their spirituals: "Ole Satan's church is here below, Up to God's free church I hope to go." In James Cone's general analysis of the spirituals, the word "Satan" was used as an equivalent for human bondage: "To be free *from* Satan meant to be free *for* Jesus, who was God making liberation a historical reality. Anyone who was not for the Kingdom, as present in the liberating work of Jesus, was automatically for Satan, who stood for enslavement."[165] The words of the song reveal much about the theological perspective of enslaved believers.[166] But the words are flat on a written page. I, for one, wish we could hear the tone of the song and catch the deep-seated grief expressed in this communal mourning.[167]

Jacobs's Samaritan . . . as a Slave

Within the context of Jacobs's description of the church during slavery, the author recalls the Luke 10 passage: "Many of them are sincere, and nearer to the gate of heaven than sanctimonious Mr. Pike, and other long-faced Christians, who see *wounded Samaritans*, and *pass by on the other side*."[168]

Jacobs's reversal of the characters in Jesus's story might seem odd at first—that is, the Samaritan becomes the "wounded" one in need of assistance in her account. Was this intentional on Jacobs's part? Or was this a slip, her memory playing a trick on her? We will take up these questions below, when looking at the use of the Samaritan character in the broader freedom-narrative tradition. Here in its present literary context, Jacobs equates Pike and the white

165. Cone, *Spirituals and the Blues*, 72.
166. Jacobs, *Incidents*, 109. The preposition "up" would have had a double meaning for many of the enslaved, as an allusion to the North (i.e., freedom).
167. Jacobs discusses several themes in the church-and-slavery chapter (111–15), including a customary section in the narratives on the difference between true and false Christianity: "There is a great difference between Christianity and religion at the south" (115).
168. Jacobs, *Incidents*, 107 (my italics).

constable leader of the testimony service with the priest and Levite who "pass by on the other side," a phrase directly from the KJV's translation of Jesus's story. Because she conflates the Samaritan with the victim from the original story, her Samaritan requires help. In Jesus's parable, the Samaritan is his imaginative choice for the hero of the story. In Jacobs's reuse of this parable, "the wounded Samaritan" is exemplified in the grieving mother whose children have been violently removed from her grasp. Just as Pike's sermons were unable to sooth the soul, so the unnamed white constable was unable to comfort the enslaved mother who had witnessed the devastating dismantling of her family. With this rhetorical switch, Jacobs associates the "wounded Samaritan" with the enslaved. What a twist to an old, familiar story!

Jacobs identifies with the "wounded Samaritan" in ways that others (e.g., Thurman, Cardenal) expected their audiences to identify with Jesus's *good* Samaritan. Jesus's Samaritan was on a journey and was relatively free to do so. But Jacobs's observation acknowledges that circumstances may hinder one's ability to act justly in a given situation. As she puts it in *Incidents*, "I feel that the slave woman ought not to be judged by the same standard as others."[169] In her case, in order to prevent continual sexual harassment from her master, she decided to have children out of wedlock—since a legal marriage was unavailable to her—with a white man, and this decision stood behind her moral reflection.

She concludes the chapter on the church and slavery with an ecclesial critique of the white Christianity she had experienced, followed by a more personal reflection on her own situation. Her final example that illustrates the "religion of the South" as distinct from "the Christianity of Christ," as Frederick Douglass would put it,[170] is one of sexual exploitation of the black female body: "If a pastor has offspring by a woman not his wife, the church dismiss [sic] him,

169. Jacobs, *Incidents*, 86.
170. Douglass, *Narrative of the Life of Frederick Douglass*, 118. See chap. 1 for a discussion on Douglass's distinction.

if she is a white woman; but if she is colored, it does not hinder his continuing to be their good shepherd."[171] If these were the ministerial expectations in Edenton, North Carolina, then it comes as no surprise that Dr. Flint (her "master"), who had recently become a member of the local church, continued to seek "Linda" out sexually despite his married status.[172] This Jacobs story offered to a public audience her own Me Too moment:

> "You can do what I require; and if you are faithful to me, you will be as virtuous as my wife," he [Dr. Flint] replied.
> I [Linda Brent] answered that the Bible didn't say so.
> His voice became hoarse with rage. "How dare you preach to me about your infernal Bible!" he exclaimed. "What right have you, who are my negro, to talk to me about what you would like, and what you wouldn't like? I am your master, and you shall obey me."
> No wonder the slaves sing,—
>
> > "Ole Satan's church is here below;
> > Up to God's free church I hope to go."[173]

Sharon Carson analyzes Jacobs's Bible defense as "the most significant theological and political passage in the entire narrative. . . . Jacobs makes a radical claim to a hermeneutics of religious and political freedom."[174] Furthermore, I would add, Jacobs exemplifies her rhetorical skill in the framing of this account with the same slave song recorded earlier.[175] Dr. Flint and other white Christians who devalued black bodies were members of "Satan's church," unable to assist a "wounded Samaritan" who may cross their path. So Jacobs views her own character in the story, Linda Brent, as a

171. Jacobs, *Incidents*, 115.
172. Linda was only twelve years old when she moved into the house of her "master," Dr. Flint (a.k.a. Dr. James Norcom), who had recently divorced his first wife and who, now "nearly fifty," married the sixteen-year-old Mary Horniblow. Yellin, *Harriet Jacobs: A Life*, 16.
173. Jacobs, *Incidents*, 115–16.
174. Carson, "Dismantling the House of the Lord," 66.
175. Jacobs, *Incidents*, 115–16.

wounded Samaritan in need of kind, gracious, compassionate assistance from audience members in the North. She hopes that her female audience, in particular, will be able to hear beyond the traditional Christian themes of the songs sung by the enslaved and catch the double meaning of the words as interpreted by those held in bondage.[176]

The Good Samaritan in Other Narratives

It is difficult to imagine that Jacobs would not have known Jesus's original story of how a *Samaritan* was the one who showed compassion for a person in need. To charge her with this ignorance questions the gifted, rhetorical skill she utilizes elsewhere within her narrative and with her Bible. Not only was she faithful in church attendance, but she was also a teacher of biblical literacy. As her biographer notes, for seven years Jacobs "pored over" biblical passages "in her attic hiding place."[177] Furthermore, her editor, Lydia Maria Childs, would have more than likely pointed out to her this obvious scriptural misstep.

As an avid reader of the narratives of other formerly enslaved people,[178] Jacobs would have also run into the more traditional reading of the good Samaritan story elsewhere. Solomon Northup—whose story was recently portrayed in the film *12 Years a Slave*, which is based on Northup's 1853 narrative—relayed that when he received a much-needed meal, it was like pouring "oil and the wine which the Good Samaritan in the 'Great Pine Woods' was ready to pour into the wounded spirit of the slave."[179] Or Douglass's multiple uses of the good Samaritan as an analogy for Sandy, a black man who gives him the "root" to help him fight off Covey, or for Miss Lucretia, a

---

176. In Carson's analysis, the "double-voice" nature of the song would allow the enslaved to sing traditional Christian themes while simultaneously offering a more radical critique of white Christianity ("Dismantling the House of the Lord," 64).

177. Yellin, *Harriet Jacobs: A Life*, 145.

178. See Yellin, *Harriet Jacobs: A Life*, 102–3.

179. Northup, *Twelve Years a Slave*, 144–45.

white woman who "bound up my head" in his 1855 account, *My Bondage and My Freedom*.[180]

Over against these earlier retellings within the narrative tradition, Jacobs's twist on the familiar parable associated the Samaritan—who was despised in Jesus's cultural context—with the one most in need of assistance in her day: the enslaved. Her Samaritan was not one who acted but was one who, like the wounded of the original story, longed to receive the helpful actions of others, which was indicative of the lives of the enslaved. Her story was a story about human agency in the midst of controlled contexts—often violently managed.

Katherine McKittrick wisely conjectures that Jacobs's time in isolation allowed her to develop the hermeneutical creativity that comes from living in a garret. For McKittrick, the garret allowed Linda Brent to see and not be seen: "She is also not unlike a disembodied master-eye, seeing from nowhere."[181] It gave Jacobs the opportunity to reimagine her limited world in unlimited ways. For her own mental well-being, Linda desperately needed to have physical distance from Dr. Flint's gaze. But over an extended period of time, the garret became a complicated space as well. From inside the garret, "there is both a separation from and connection to the world outside the attic; she is both inside and outside, captive and free."[182] Inside this secret hiding space, Jacobs could attend to two worlds simultaneously and witness her surroundings that were "captive and free." Furthermore, because she was semitrapped in this space for seven years, the garret becomes a symbol of the nature of slavery on individuals and communities: "The garret locates her in and amongst the irrational workings of slavery as a witness, participant, and fugitive."[183]

Despite the cramped quarters, the physically confined space allowed her to (re)view her enslaved context from another vantage

---

180. Douglass, *My Bondage and My Freedom*, 239, 130, respectively. Neither story appeared in Douglass's initial story from ten years earlier, *Narrative of the Life of Frederick Douglass*.

181. McKittrick, *Demonic Grounds*, 43.

182. McKittrick, *Demonic Grounds*, 42.

183. McKittrick, *Demonic Grounds*, 42.

point; it also allowed her to think differently about her God and her Bible. Whatever we might think of how Jacobs imagined her wounded Samaritan,[184] her creative hermeneutical decision to attach this character to the most vulnerable of her day was one way to make relevant the biblical stories of her faith. Despite writing from the perspective of one now freed, she still recognized that many enslaved victims needed public, national action. Hers was not a personal tale but a broader one. As long as one person was still enslaved, Jacobs would challenge the institutional system of bondage in the land.

We would be remiss to overemphasize the wounded-Samaritan motif as reflective only of Jacobs's individual life. In fact, to do so would misrepresent a key ingredient in the narrative, a feature that distinguished her literary art from that of her male counterparts: the role of the community.[185] Her life was not limited to the printed text; she opened an antislavery reading room,[186] founded a school for African American children, and raised funds for housing facilities, an orphanage, and an elderly care facility.[187] The activism of this "wounded Samaritan" embodied most fully what it meant to be a neighbor.[188] The "wound" her Samaritan faced was one the community bore and one the community would help alleviate, just as her grandmother and many other individuals—including several white folks (who were not abolitionists)—assisted in her fight against Dr. Flint by maintaining the secrecy of her hideout, the assistance from the North (sending letters on her behalf, as if from her), and eventually the escape.

184. Why did Jacobs not find the enslaved in the victim—the one who fell among thieves?

185. Braxton, *Black Women Writing Autobiography*, 20.

186. She opened this room with her brother (John Jacobs) on the floor above Frederick Douglass's newspaper office (Yellin, "Texts and Contexts," 264).

187. She traveled to England to raise funds by selling her narrative under the title *The Deeper Wrong*.

188. She assisted in the care and development of many of the formerly enslaved in Alexandria, Boston, and Savannah. If, in Jacobs's "tradition," she had ever heard that "Christ" was the Samaritan (allegorically), then, again, she is indirectly associating Christ with the enslaved.

Summary

To the lawyer's opening query, Jesus replied, "How do you read?" Indeed, the way one reads the Bible defines and determines the way a person thinks about life and vice versa. Jacobs had her own reading of the Samaritan story, and it was one in which she conflated two victims from the original story—the one who fell into the hands of the robbers and the Samaritan who was despised in his own cultural setting as an enemy of the Jews—with a third "victim," one she knew intimately well. Though she was unable to count on the white Christian community during her Southern enslavement (except, perhaps, for one white mistress slaveholder who hid her for several weeks before she went to her grandmother's attic),[189] to count on her grandmother's theological view of God's ordained providence, or to count on Mr. Sands (with whom she had two children) to seek her freedom, she appealed to her female Northern audience members to "Rise up, ye women!" and assist the "wounded Samaritan" and not "to pass by on the other side."

▧ Conclusion

Saint Augustine, Howard Thurman, the Solentiname Community, and Harriet Jacobs each represent four distinct settings. Nonetheless, they share an interest in the parable of the merciful Samaritan as a productive resource for the thinking and growth of their respective communities. Whatever method he utilized, Augustine found love to be central to the hermeneutical task, so he discovered in these verses the grand story of God's love for humanity. In that divine-human encounter, the Samaritan represents the Christ figure himself, the epitome of love. Although love was key for Thurman as well, the mid-twentieth-century mystic ascertained from this parable a humanizing

---

189. Also, her white "lover" (Mr. Sands) could be mentioned. Although she eventually and apparently willingly had two children with him, Jacobs had a complicated relationship with this neighbor friend.

tale, a story that allows interpreters an opportunity to speak more clearly about the human experience as they encounter people unlike themselves. For Thurman, the human-human encounter lies at the heart of this first-century parable, especially as racial tensions remained at the forefront of this contemporary prophet's concerns. The Solentiname community would uncover from these verses an opportunity to place the spiritual, communal practice of Bible study alongside communal reflection on their political situation. For this South American ecclesial gathering, the hero of the parable had to be one who stood on the side of the politically oppressed of present-day Nicaragua. Finally, in a less direct analysis of the parable story, Jacobs reimagined the role of the Samaritan for her contemporary audience. For this creative storyteller, the hero of Jesus's parable (overlapped with the wounded figure) is reconceived as an analogy for the enslaved in her day, a hero in desperate need of assistance from any northern sisters who would intervene in the human-bondage struggle of their day. The approaches to the biblical story of all four interpreters differ as much as the conclusions they draw, but they all recognize the power of one of Jesus's greatest parables on the shape and practices of the lives of people who wrestle with biblical stories to engage with their worlds. These dynamic examples each show us what it means to employ a biblical parable afresh in new settings and times. We do well to follow their lead.

3

Mercy and the Neighbor

Reading the Parable

The identity of the author of the Gospel of Luke remains uncertain. There is no consensus within biblical scholarship. Moreover, whether the author was Jewish continues to be debated.[1] This is no less true for the author of one of Luke's sources, the Gospel of Mark.[2] This unknown factor is not unimportant to the overall story or to the particular concern of this chapter. If we knew with certainty the ethnic identity of the author, then we would have the capacity to see how a gentile believer (or a Hellenistic Jewish believer) might retell the story of the Jewish Jesus in ways distinct from his fellow Jewish believers (assuming the authors of the other Gospels were Jewish). What is clear from the written text is that the audience was an ethnically

1. Some support Luke's non-Jewish identity; e.g., Vinson in *Luke*, 3; and Karris, "Gospel according to Luke," 675. For others, the identity remains unknown; e.g., Ringe, *Luke*, 19; and Lieu, *Gospel of Luke*, xv.
2. The debate over the (Jewish?) authorship of the second Gospel continues as well; see Wills, "Mark," 67–68; also Collins, *Mark*, 2–6. The author of the Third Gospel states his dependence on earlier, unnamed sources (Luke 1:1–4)—one of which may have been the Gospel of Mark.

mixed congregation with a growing gentile presence.[3] To appeal to this Jewish-gentile Christian community, how did "Luke"[4] report the events of Jesus's life and mission in a way that would validate gentile sensibilities? To put it another way, how *Jewish* was Luke's Jesus and how did Luke communicate that Jewishness for the non-Jewish members of his audience?[5]

Luke clearly underscores that Jesus is Jewish. He mentions Jesus's circumcision (2:21), Jesus's childhood training among Jerusalem teachers (2:42–49), the opening announcement of Jesus's mission at his hometown synagogue (4:16–30), and his regular participation in various Jewish meal gatherings (5:27–32; 7:36–50; 11:37–41; 14:1–24). With the exception of the last item, the other Gospels do not report these events. Luke methodically emphasizes the Jewishness of Jesus for his audience.

Luke's stories about Jesus's attention to the margins of society— women, children, the sick, the poor—refer to accounts about individuals within Jewish circles. Contemporary Christian readers should not interpret Luke's account as a critique of Jewish practices toward those on the margins. Luke's Jesus stands firmly within the Judaism of his day and continues alongside other Jewish people who care for those on the fringes of society, economically or socially. After all, note how some Jewish parents (or perhaps custodians) seek out Jesus's blessing of their children.

When reading stories about Jesus's critique of other Jewish leaders, one of the challenges is to recognize that these stories now reside within a larger account directed to a *gentile*-leaning audience.

3. See Nadella, *Dialogue Not Dogma*, 121–25.

4. The traditional label of the author of the Gospel of Luke ("Luke") will be used throughout this book without implying any historical information (outside the text) about the person who may have written this story. On Luke's gentile audience, see the standard introductions to the New Testament (e.g., Powell, *Introducing the New Testament*, 161–81).

5. One way might be to omit Jesus's Aramaic words, which Matthew and Mark record. Luke omits the Aramaic from his source, the Gospel of Mark, at the parallel passages (cf. Mark 3:17 // Luke 6:14; Mark 5:41 // Luke 8:54; Mark 10:46 // Luke 18:35; Mark 14:36 // Luke 22:42; Mark 15:22 // Luke 23:33; Mark 15:34 // Luke 23:45–46).

They can easily become misinterpreted as anti-Jewish accounts and utilized for anti-Semitic purposes today. So we do well to remember how Jewish Luke's Jesus is!

What It Might (Have) Mean(t)[6]

The Dialogue: The Outer Story (10:25–29)

The basic message of Luke's story surrounding the parable is straightforward, but some of the minor details of the narrative deserve attention. In brief, a lawyer approaches Jesus and inquires about how to inherit eternal life. Jesus responds with his own question about Torah: "What is written in the law?" (10:26). The lawyer (Gk. *nomikos*) was an expert in the law (Gk. *nomos*). Consequently, Jesus appeals to the lawyer's expertise, though any law-abiding Jew should know the answer to what is written in Torah: "love God and love neighbor." At least the lawyer understood that he must be about the "doing" of the faith: "What must I *do* . . . ?" (10:25).

Even though the man knew *what* was in Torah, he was still questioning *how* to understand it ("Who is my neighbor?" [10:29]). Leviticus seems explicit in how it defines the neighbor, even while opening up questions about self-love: "Love your neighbor as yourself" (Lev. 19:18). How does one love and treat oneself? Unless they are masochistic, most people care deeply about their personal well-being. This, then, is how one should treat the neighbor. But understanding "love" is not the lawyer's concern. Rather, it is identifying the "neighbor" that troubles him. It is, after all, a fair question.

The fuller context of the chapter in Leviticus provides some clues. In Leviticus "neighbor" undoubtedly refers to other members of the covenant community. Yet this principle could also be extended to

---

6. I chose this heading in the spirit of Brian Blount's 2018 SBL presidential address. Interpretations of the Bible have traditionally been divided into two distinct categories—"what the text *meant*" and "what the text *means*"—but because contemporary readers are unable to remove their own bias fully, interpretations should be viewed as "what the text means" and "what the text means" ("Souls of Biblical Folks").

those persons who were not members of Israel. For example, a few verses after 19:18, the law places the "immigrant" into the position of the "neighbor": "When immigrants live in your land with you, you must not cheat them. Any immigrant who lives with you must be treated as if they were one of your citizens. You must love them as yourself, because you were immigrants in the land of Egypt; I am the LORD your God" (Lev. 19:33–34 CEB). But perhaps this lawyer was an atomistic type of reader; that is, he read narrowly into each verse rather than connecting the verse to its broader literary context. Must the meaning of "neighbor" be defined by its meaning *within its original historical or literary context* and not by what "neighbor" might mean decades and centuries later? Does each generation have the responsibility to redefine who the neighbor is? Perhaps this is what has motivated the lawyer's question. Who really counts as a neighbor in the first century? Who counts as an immigrant? Does the category of the immigrant-neighbor change in cultural time and space?

Moving forward in the dialogue with the lawyer, Jesus's position becomes magnified with his second question: "How do you read?" (Luke 10:26). The NRSV translates the phrase as "What do you read there?" which functions as a further elucidation of the opening question, "What is written in the law?" Other English translations—in particular the CEB, NIV, and ESV—all seem to catch the more hermeneutical intent of the Greek question, *pōs anaginōskeis* (*How* do you read/interpret it?). It is not simply *what* one reads; it is *how* one reads it. Following the lawyer's response of loving God and neighbor and Jesus's affirmation of this answer, the lawyer then asks a second question: "Who is my neighbor?" Jesus replies with a parable, an example of how he will interpret the meaning of "neighbor." The lawyer clearly knows what is in Torah. The deeper question is whether his understanding will allow for an expansion of his reading practices.

The narrator then intervenes more directly in the telling of the story (10:29). The opening four verses (vv. 25–28) provide straightforward dialogue between Jesus and his interlocutor, with the exception of the initial opening narrative aside that this was a kind of (sincere?) "test." But after this tête-à-tête with Jesus, the lawyer's next question is preceded by the narrator's qualification: the lawyer desired "to justify himself" (v. 29). What exactly did he wish to "justify"? *His* view of the neighbor? His *way* of living in the world? Or was he attempting to justify his initial stance, that this was all merely a test to determine—in light of verses 21–24—Jesus's credentials (see v. 25)?[7] Before we enter the story within the story (i.e., the parable), let us review briefly the Gospel of Luke's narrative placement of the scene of Jesus's encounter with this *nomikos*.

What Precedes the Parable

The lawyer's appearance is abrupt in the Lukan narrative. At 10:17, Jesus addresses seventy of his disciples who have returned from a short mission.[8] At verse 23, Jesus addresses the twelve disciples, praising them for their ability to "see," a signal that they were able to read the contemporary situation well. Luke's Jesus emphasizes God's sovereignty to reveal the mystery to whomever God wishes, and the Twelve (and the seventy?) benefited from this revelation. Private moments between Jesus and his followers are rare in Luke's narrative (v. 23).[9] At verse 25, seemingly out of nowhere, the inquisitive lawyer appears. Within the narrative sequence, the lawyer is unwilling to interpret Scripture for the contemporary moment on his own, so he seeks Jesus's additional teaching.[10] By the end of the account,

7. As John Nolland puts it, "The lawyer comes to test the credentials of this One who claims to speak the mind of God" (*Luke 9:21–18:34*, 585). Preceded in the narrative by Satan's test (Luke 4:2, 12), the lawyer's test may have been disingenuous.

8. At Luke 10:17 (and at 10:1), there is a text-critical distinction; some ancient manuscripts offer the number seventy-two.

9. In Luke, Jesus instructs the disciples privately only here and at 9:10, unlike the multiple occurrences in the Gospel of Mark (cf. Mark 4:34; 6:32; 9:2, 28; 13:3).

10. Following Jesus's death and resurrection, the disciples, too, will need hermeneutical assistance: "Then, he opened their minds to understand the Scriptures" (Luke 24:45).

he grasps the point that Jesus intends (v. 37). Whether he followed through in any practical way is left up to the audience's imagination.

What Follows the Parable

Luke 10:38–42 leads us to another point of comparison: the story about two sisters who follow Jesus. From Luke's description, Martha "welcomes" him and Mary "listens" to his teaching. In the Lukan narrative, these sisters appear to be disciples of some kind, people who have at least sufficient resources to be supportive of his mission, so they offer sustenance for the journey (cf. 8:1–3). We may presume that the sisters are simply friends of Jesus's family, people with whom he grew up. But the story is not focused on the teacher's well-being. It turns the reader's attention elsewhere.

How important is the Martha-Mary story for understanding the Samaritan parable? Does it shed narrative light on the previous story? Are these two stories—as John Nolland suggests[11]—two distinct examples of loving God (Mary's act of listening) and loving neighbor (the Samaritan's act of doing)? Or are these two stories more *similar* in function, as two of Luke's examples of "the relationship between hospitality and ministry," as Stephanie Buckhanon Crowder contends?[12] Does Luke have a larger narrative purpose in attaching the Samaritan-as-hero account to a story in which two Jewish women are disciples? Is there a juxtaposition between the Samaritan who "demonstrated mercy" (whom Jesus praises) and Mary, who has "chosen the better part" (10:42)? Is there a narrative link between the innkeeper and Martha, who receives Jesus and cares for his needs (v. 38)?[13] If so, do readers need to revisit the significant work of the innkeeper, which we will discuss below, or was the elevation of Mary's action a narrative commentary on the Samaritan's initial act? Finally, if the audience should hear these two stories in conjunction with

11. Nolland, *Luke 9:21–18:34*, 605.
12. Crowder, "Luke," 170.
13. Strikingly, this one (Jesus) in need of "care" then becomes the one teaching Mary.

each other, has Jesus now become the "victim" in need of care? This second story potentially opens up a lot of interpretive possibilities that are worth pursuing in light of the narrative placement of Jesus's dialogue with the lawyer.

One Other Narrative Point of Comparison

Within Luke's overall story about Jesus, this lawyer is not the only person to ask Jesus the initial question "What must I do to inherit eternal life?"[14] Both a lawyer and a wealthy ruler call Jesus "teacher" and ask "What should I do?" (18:18), for which Jesus provides necessary advice.[15] While there are no parallels in the other Gospels for the Luke 10 parable, Mark and Matthew provide parallels for the account of the rich ruler (Luke 18:18–30 // Mark 10:17–31 // Matt. 19:16–30). As a good Jewish teacher, Jesus points each of his inquisitors to Torah, the commandments, and not—as some contemporary Christians might think—to himself. In addition, he asks only the lawyer, "How do you read [it]?" Lawyers and rulers alike were both Torah-observant Jews, but there was much more to these encounters.

Their distinct reactions take their engagements in divergent directions. The lawyer's follow-up question ("Who is my neighbor?") is replaced by the ruler's more confident statement: "I have kept all these [commandments] since my youth" (Luke 18:21). Yet in Luke's narrative construction, both still lack something. The lawyer's question provokes Jesus's parable of the Samaritan. The parable, then, allows the lawyer to draw his own conclusion and to determine his own actions. As a later midrash stipulates, "So the parable should not be lightly esteemed in your eyes, since by means of the parable

14. Since the 1980s we have recognized that "parables cast light upon the narrative, but they also should be interpreted in light of the narrative" (David Gowler's description of John Drury's work; see Gowler, *What Are They Saying*, 35).

15. The rich man's primary inquiry gets sidetracked momentarily when Jesus questions his description of Jesus as "good" (Luke 18:19). Matthew's parallel—"What good must I do?"—avoids the aside (Matt. 19:16).

a [person] arrives at the true meaning of the words of the Torah" (Song of Songs Rabbah 1:1 §8).[16] However, Jesus gives a more forceful and direct charge to the ruler: "Sell everything and give it away to the poor" (18:22)—an activity partially exemplified by the Samaritan's action within the parable. The qualification of the individual ruler's sadness is more conclusive than Luke's omission of the lawyer's reaction. Luke's ruler is unwilling (and perhaps unable, due to family obligations) to carry out Jesus's demand.[17] Unlike his narrative counterpart, the lawyer is not confronted directly with the poor (or the abused) but with a Samaritan.[18] His imagination is prodded, not his purse.

The Parable: The Inner Story (10:30–35)

As chapter 2 has shown, the parable proper has attracted the attention of interpreters throughout the ages. Interpreters frequently encounter the familiar parable without attention to its setting, but this parable, similar to many others, has a literary context. Whether this narrative context is the actual historical one is less important for our purposes than wrestling with Luke's intentional narrative work here. Luke's context includes the lawyer's inquiry. But more than that, Jesus tells this parable to explore the lawyer's question about defining the neighbor and thereby also addresses, indirectly, the initial question ("What must I do?"). The story has *five* subject characters (that is, characters associated with specific action verbs): a man who travels from Jerusalem to Jericho, the thieves who attack him and leave him half dead, a priest who travels that road and passes by on the other side, a Levite who follows the priest's path, and finally, a

16. Translation from Freedman and Simon, *Midrash Rabbah*, quoted in Snodgrass, *Stories with Intent*, 112. Midrash is a type of ancient Jewish biblical commentary that arguably began during the early centuries CE.

17. Only Mark depicts Jesus's love for the ruler (Mark 10:21).

18. The Samaritan is using his funds to assist someone; he is not, presumably, giving it all away. Even then, both stories seem to make a similar point: utilize one's possessions for those in need.

Samaritan who also travels that road and shows compassion. Other characters—for example, the innkeeper—are not listed here because Luke did not connect any action verb to them.[19] Of course, there are other unmentioned "characters"—for example, the spouse of the innkeeper, the family members of the victim, or the business partners of the Samaritan—who lie in the background of the tragedy and the eventual positive outcome of this story.[20]

On word count alone, it is easy to determine who the main character is. Jesus relays the entire parable in 105 (or possibly 106) words.[21] Of those words, he describes the victim's crisis in only twenty Greek words (10:30). It takes only an additional twenty-five to twenty-six words to explain the priest's and Levite's reactions (vv. 31–32). More than half (sixty words!) of the words of the entire parable are reserved for the Samaritan's response (vv. 33–35).[22] The Samaritan's compassion is extoled in various action steps: he bandages wounds, brings the man to an inn on his mule, cares for him at the inn, pays two denarii for additional care, and then, finally, communicates with the innkeeper. The Samaritan is the only one to speak within the parable proper. More than half of Jesus's words in this short parable emphasize the Samaritan's activities toward this stranger and thereby answer the lawyer's question. But is there more to the story?

First, despite the headings in many English Bibles, Jesus never calls the Samaritan "good." It is not an adjective used to describe

19. In an indirect challenge to the idea here, Bruce Longenecker elevates the innkeeper's role as fundamental to a more thorough understanding of the parable, in "Story of the Samaritan and the Innkeeper."

20. Each of these imagined characters would play some role in a situation of this kind. For example, the innkeeper's spouse would provide meals (and care) for her family and this uninvited guest.

21. Some ancient manuscripts add one Greek word—*genomenos*—to 10:32, which would add emphasis to a stage in life of "becoming" a Levite. Compare the similar usage of this Greek participle associated with those "*who had become* servants of the word" in Luke 1:2.

22. In English, using the NRSV as our base text, the word counts appear as follows: victim's crisis = twenty-eight words; reactions of the priest and Levite = forty-one words; the Samaritan's response = eighty-three words.

any human in Luke's narrative. For Luke's Jesus, "no one is good but God alone" (Luke 18:19).[23] While the Samaritan's action could have been described as a "good" act—indeed, it was described as an act of mercy by the lawyer—Jesus never labels it "good," a term that carries important theological meaning for Luke. Rather, for Jesus it seems this act of kindness was the only appropriate, fitting, humane action—that is, to treat another person in critical need the way one would wish to be treated. So it was not just a good act; it was the *only* way any human being ought to act toward another person. Other actions—"to pass by on the other side," for example—could then be classified as inhumane acts (i.e., the failure to act), what James might describe as sins of omission (James 4:17). The idea is also present in Proverbs (and elsewhere): "Do not withhold good from those to whom it is due, when it is in your power to do it" (Prov. 3:27 NRSV).[24] For Jesus this story represents what it means to follow the Levitical command to "love your neighbor as yourself." His parable is an illustration of the Levitical teaching, albeit with a twist. The naming of the Samaritan was a (slight?) modification on what might be expected (i.e., a priest, a Levite, or a common Jewish person).

Second, the Greek verb *splanchnizomai* (Luke 10:33) is a key word for understanding the story. The English translations differ, some leaning in the direction of expressing "pity" (NRSV, NIV) and others preferring to express its equivalent as "compassion" (KJV, CEB, ESV). There may be subtle distinctions that are worth examining.[25] "Pity" is usually associated with feelings of *sympathy* for another person and may not contain the impetus to assist; "compassion" is usually associated with feelings of *empathy* for another person and

23. This parallels Mark's account (Mark 10:18). Matthew shifts the adjective "good" from the address ("good teacher") to the question ("What good deed must I do?"; Matt. 19:16).

24. The language "You may not withhold your help" is present in the Torah (Deut. 24:14–15). In the proverb and in Deuteronomy, the context includes the "neighbor."

25. The NRSV reserves "mercy" language for its translation of the verb *eleeō* (cf. Luke 16:24; 18:38–39).

generally includes a desire to assist another person.[26] If this linguistic distinction holds true in a practical manner, compassion is more than an emotion; it is an emotion that instigates action. In fact, some may innocently misinterpret compassion as pity, until action occurs. Pity may be associated with negative feelings toward the other or the other's situation; compassion is related more closely to love and thereby usually does not include negative feelings or judgment toward the other.[27] Pity may cause a person to feel sorrow at a given situation; compassion forces one to stand up and do something. Some people witness unjust treatment of others, and it moves them to protest with their physical bodies. Most of us may sympathize, but we do not place our bodies, time, or energy on the line.[28]

If some part of this linguistic distinction is in the background, the NRSV's translation, "He was moved with pity," may cause readers to misunderstand the Samaritan's emotion. This description of the difference between these two terms implies that pity is not sufficient to move a person to action; if that is the case, and in light of the Greek word usage elsewhere (Luke 7:13; 15:20), the preferable translation is "compassion."[29] This distinction may also allow us to view the actions of the other characters in more sympathetic ways. "Passing by on the other side" may not be an inhumane act after all; it may merely be an expression of pity: "I see his condition, but I am unable, bodily, to do anything at this moment to assist him."[30] In light of this distinction,

26. The passive form of the Greek verb in Luke 10:33 here—"he was filled up with compassion"—may imply a biological element. Recent studies have shown that there is a connection between compassion and biology. Keltner, "Compassionate Instinct."

27. Emelda M., "Difference between Pity and Compassion."

28. James Cone's harsh critique of Reinhold Niebuhr may be a fitting analogy here: "Niebuhr had 'eyes to see' black suffering, but I believe he lacked the 'heart to feel' it as his own" (Cross and the Lynching Tree, 41).

29. The NRSV translates the Greek splanchnizomai as "compassion" in Luke 7:13; 15:20.

30. As Amy-Jill Levine emphasizes, any priest committed to his profession would stop to care for the body (Short Stories by Jesus, 99–100). The parable is unclear whether the priest or Levite saw a "half-dead" body, which led to Howard Thurman's conclusion that the priest did not really notice the condition of the beaten man at all (see chap. 2).

the parable could be called "The Compassionate Samaritan" or "The Committed Samaritan" or even "The Priest's or Levite's Pity." Do any of us have enough compassion to act in this manner—to alter our plans and commit even beyond the immediate need as the Samaritan did—toward other human beings who have fallen into crisis? Human pity is natural; human compassion is unconventional.

Third, what distinguishes the Samaritan from his traveling counterparts is that when he sees the beaten man, he expresses a more favorable emotion toward the victim's situation that causes him to act (Luke 10:33). Luke describes the Samaritan's emotional state with the Greek verb *esplanchnisthē*, the passive form of the verb *splanchnizomai*, indicating that the victim's condition moved the Samaritan's inner emotions (the *splanchna*, the "guts"), which then moved him to action. In the Third Gospel, this characterization is crucial, as Luke uses this Greek verbal form on only three distinct occasions, each one associated with a similar outcome: the one who is moved assists an individual to return to health and wholeness. Two examples appear in parables. The Samaritan in our present story (10:33) is followed by a later parable in which a Jewish father witnesses his son's shameful return home but then warmly greets him with compassion and acts on his son's behalf to restore him to the family fold (15:20). Outside of the parables, Luke reserves the verb to describe the action of Jesus in Luke 7. Because of compassion, Jesus raises a son to life after witnessing his mother's grief (v. 13). In addition, the noun form is used only once, in a prophecy in which John the Baptist is the primary focal point, to describe God's own *splanchna eleous*, "deep compassion" (CEB) or "tender mercy" (KJV; NRSV), in providing a way of salvation for Israel (1:78). With the use of this language, Luke places the Samaritan in good literary company.

Fourth, the original readers of Luke's Gospel would have been unprepared for the indifferent priest within the parable. It is the only time Jesus mentions a priest as a character in one of his parables. Moreover, in Luke and Acts common priests tend to be positive figures. In the larger narrative account, Luke seems to make a distinction between general priests (*hiereis*) and the chief priests (*archiereis*; associated with the Jerusalem temple). The latter group is antagonistic to Jesus and actively conspires with others for his removal after he arrives in Jerusalem (Luke 19:47; 22:2–4, 52–54). The general priesthood, on the other hand, has less tension with Jesus, if any at all. The Gospel of Luke opens with the righteous priest Zechariah, the father of John the Baptist, a sympathetic character (1:5–66). On two separate occasions, Jesus sends individuals to priests to confirm their cleanliness after their healings (5:14; 17:14), the common custom according to Leviticus 13. The references to priests in Acts continue this trend. Despite initial tensions between temple priests and Peter and John over their teaching about resurrection (Acts 4:1), a number of Jerusalem priests eventually become "obedient to the faith" (6:7). Some priests oppose the Jesus movement; other priests join it.

The Luke 10 parable is not a statement about the general priesthood or the absence of compassion among Jews. Sadly, with the rise of anti-Semitism again in our particular context, this reminder is necessary.[31] Jesus and the lawyer (who recognizes mercy when he sees it) were both Jews. By implication, this parable may be the Lukan Jesus's critique of religious leaders associated with the Jerusalem temple. Even here, readers should proceed cautiously since Luke's narrative does not generally take an antitemple stance.[32] Luke is writing in the aftermath of the temple's destruction (ca. 70 CE), even while situating his characters two generations earlier. Stephen's speech, for example, which seems to critique the physical temple (Acts 7:48), may be a sentiment—in Luke's narrative (world)—about life after the recent

31. Miller, "Anti-Semitism Is on the Rise."
32. Cf. Fuller, *Restoration of Israel*, 266–68. On Luke's complicated position toward the temple, Fuller recognizes the following: "Although Luke portrays the temple positively, in its associations with Jesus and the formative Christian community, . . . nowhere does the author indicate that a new Temple will be a feature of Israel's eschatological restoration" (266n278). Again Fuller writes, "Luke indicates little interest in developing a Temple-centered understanding of restoration" (268). For more on this more multifaceted view, see also Brawley, *Luke-Acts and the Jews*, 107–32.

destruction of the temple, although scholars debate whether Luke shares the position the character Stephen articulates.[33] Indeed, the entire Gospel ends with a declaration that Jesus's followers remained in the temple giving blessings to God (Luke 24:53). Additionally, according to Acts, after Jesus's departure the temple was a gathering place for the developing community (2:46), as many of them went up daily for the temple prayers (3:1). The parable is not, generally, a story about a "Jesus" who stands over against "Judaism" (i.e., against Torah; against temple). To interpret the account from this perspective distorts the meaning of the parable. Taking this approach as a reading strategy has implications for the broader questions central to this account: "Who is my neighbor?" and "How do you read?"

To appreciate the reversal of expectations inherent to the parable—as Jesus often intended in his parables—it is key to recognize the following: (1) A Samaritan, whose interactions with Jews were generally negative (see below),[34] was depicted positively within the parable. (2) A priest, whose interactions with Jews were generally positive, was depicted negatively within the parable.[35] It is a parable after all!

Finally, the Samaritan of Jesus's parable is an imagined character. Within the parables, it is uncustomary for the Jewish Jesus to imagine a non-Jewish character. It is a Jewish shepherd who tracks down his wayward sheep (Luke 15:3–7); it is a Jewish woman who diligently searches for her lost coin (vv. 8–10); it is a Jewish father who expresses compassion for his wayward son (vv. 11–32). Another way to think about such characters within parables is to recognize the

33. For Shaye Cohen, Luke's position on the temple should be interpreted in light of his "idealized" portrayal to define the movement as its own separate (i.e., sectarian) group. *From the Maccabees to the Mishnah*, 160–61.

34. In the Gospel of John, Jesus's interaction with a Samaritan woman is tense, partly because "Jews do not share things in common with Samaritans" (John 4:9 NRSV).

35. There is little information on Levites within the Luke-Acts narrative. A Levite named Joseph Barnabas joins the followers of Jesus (Acts 4:36) and eventually becomes Paul's mentor.

Samaritan as a stock character. Among parable interpreters, there is a debate about how well parables reveal the reality of first-century life. Compare, for example, the parable of the Pharisee and the tax collector, who are depicted as individuals who offer prayers at the temple (18:9–14). Jesus's audience was much more likely to meet a humble Pharisee than they would an unassuming collector. That reversal is what makes the parable work.[36]

Let us assume that the parable of Luke 10 discloses little about any flesh-and-blood Samaritan who may have lived in the region. When we read about flesh-and-blood types within the confines of Luke's narrative world, we read about Samaritans who are less than merciful: an entire village (or at least its Samaritan leaders) refuses hospitality to Jesus and his entourage, so they have to take a detour around that town (9:51–53).[37] It was common for Jews to pass through this village during major festivals in Jerusalem.[38] Presumably, the disciples would not have attempted to negotiate accommodations if it were not so. More than likely, other Jewish travelers whose faces were not "set toward Jerusalem" would have passed through without incident. Angered by this hostile rejection, some of Jesus's disciples want to retaliate; Jesus reprimands their violent desire. The Jewish historian Josephus confirms this broader tension between Jews and Samaritans within the culture, including one occasion in which the violence became so prominent that the Roman governor of Syria, Ummidius Quadratus, sent representatives of each party to Rome to plead their case to the imperial court. Eventually, Claudius Caesar (r. 41–54 CE) sided in favor of the Jews and executed the leaders of the Samaritans.[39]

Despite the larger narrative's "reality" depicting what Jesus and his disciples may have experienced firsthand, Luke's Jesus, surprisingly, imagines a merciful and attentive Samaritan. Jesus's personal

---

36. Brian Blount suggests that the reversal motif within Luke's Gospel also directly affects the social and the political. *Then the Whisper Put on Flesh*, 79.

37. "Because his face was set toward Jerusalem" (Luke 9:53 NRSV).

38. Pummer, *Samaritans*, 35; Nolland, *Luke 9:21–18:34*, 537.

39. Josephus, *J.W.* 2.232–49; *Ant.* 20.118–36.

experience of the Samaritan village's public rejection did not hinder
the Jewish teacher from offering a story in which a Samaritan functions as the hero (Luke 10:33). Nor did these tensions hinder Luke
from relaying another affirmative story—a story in which Jesus heals
ten lepers and only one, a Samaritan, returns to thank Jesus for this
act of kindness (17:12–19).[40] Along with the parable of the compassionate Samaritan, this story of the "grateful Samaritan," as it is
sometimes labeled, is also absent from the other Gospels.[41] Luke
and Jesus can imagine a world—despite their views of real flesh-
and-blood Samaritans—in which Samaritans are potential heroes
in their stories, the ones who best exemplify sensitivity to the other
and physical expressions of assistance and thanksgiving. The loss of
the imagination in theological, political, social, and ecclesial circles
is one of the greatest losses we can have. Jesus's parable pushes all
people—followers and nonfollowers alike—to imagine the other
in a way different from what our experiences, our traditions, and
our cultural biases may offer us.[42] The importance of storytelling
for challenging the storyteller's cultural peers cannot be overstated.
Howard Thurman would agree (see chap. 2)! Who are the heroes of
our stories? Do they always look like us, think like us, love like us,
or believe like us?

In this direction, Luke offers a more favorable portrayal of Samaritans than his Gospel counterparts Matthew and John.[43] In Mat-

40. Over against the other nine who failed to return, Jesus acknowledges the Samaritan as a "foreigner" (*allogenēs*; Luke 17:18). For an interpretation that suggests
a *negative* tone to Jesus's observation that only the foreigner returned, see Barreto,
"Except This Foreigner?"
41. Cf. Betz, "Cleansing of the Ten Lepers," 314. As a sidenote, it crosses centuries
and cultural borders to note how illnesses, sicknesses, and pandemics often bring
people of various viewpoints and cultural backgrounds together.
42. Reflecting on her own creative literature in a series of talks presented at Harvard University, Toni Morrison divulges her thinking on this practice: "Narrative
fiction provides a controlled wilderness, an opportunity to be and to become the
Other. The stranger. With sympathy, clarity, and the risk of self-examination" (*Origin
of Others*, 91).
43. The ethnic (geographical and religious) identity marker does not occur in
Mark, the earliest Gospel.

thew, Jesus commands his disciples to stay away from gentiles and Samaritans (Matt. 10:5);[44] in Luke's parallel, there are less specific geographical limitations (Luke 9:1–5), which is, in turn, emphasized even further when he sends out the seventy (though with a nuance) to go "to every town and place where *he intended* to go" (Luke 10:1, my italics).[45] Generally, a negative image of the Samaritan also appears in the Fourth Gospel, thus the impact of the account of Jesus's encounter with the Samaritan woman (John 4). The Jews could use the label as a cultural slur, associating the ethnic group with demonic forces: "Are we not right in saying that you are a Samaritan and have a demon?" (John 8:48 NRSV).[46] In John, the common impression that (true?) Judeans do not associate with Samaritans at all is expressed as a narrative aside (John 4:9). Yet even in the Fourth Gospel (similar to the Third Gospel in this regard) the portrayal is conflicted as the Samaritan community, encouraged by this well-known woman's positive encounter, is willing to host Jesus for a short period (John 4:40). Along these lines, Jesus is not reluctant to reach out to a Samaritan woman (John 4). On this latter point, Luke and John both move beyond Matthew's more restrictive (and perhaps more historical) portrayal of the mission of Jesus.

On the surface, Luke's Jesus seems more inclusive than Matthew's Jesus. Indeed, sometimes only the "foreigner" or the "other" (*allogenēs*)[47]—the Samaritan—responds in the appropriate manner, as did the one who formerly had leprosy (Luke 17:18). The scholarly

44. The Gospel of Matthew distinguishes Samaritans from gentiles *and* from the "house of Israel" (10:5–6).

45. Assuming there were towns in which gentiles resided, it is likely that those towns were not intended, since it took a "revelation"—as Peter's words to Cornelius imply—for Jewish followers of Jesus to begin to think about gentile inclusion: "You yourselves know that it is unlawful for a Jew to associate with or to visit a Gentile; but God has shown me that I should not call anyone profane or unclean" (Acts 10:28 NRSV).

46. In a recent challenge to the "common reading" of the Samaritan as enemy, Matthew Chalmers did not address the controversial label in John 8; see "Rethinking Luke 10."

47. The first part of this composite Greek word (*allos*) means "an-other."

consensus is that Luke wrote in a setting and time period in which non-Jews represented the predominant growth of the *ekklēsia* (church).[48] In light of that setting, Luke wished to retell the story of Jesus to account for the growth of the movement in this non-Jewish direction. Along these lines, only Luke's Jesus tells a parable in which a Samaritan plays the leading role. Likely, it is the growth of the mission in Samaria, as reported in Acts, that Luke wished to account for in the earlier stages of the Jesus mission.[49] In Luke's source, the Gospel of Mark, the terms "Samaria" and "Samaritans" do not occur at all, which compels many interpreters to assume that the historical Jesus had minimal contact with the Samaritans.[50] Luke offered a corrective in the Third Gospel in light of what he had come to know (and experience?) in the later growth of the movement. It was rewritten history to account for the ever-increasing and multiethnic movement in his day. When the adherents of a movement—or the citizens of a nation, for that matter—no longer look like or think like the earliest members of the movement, how do later advocates retell their origin story in order to maintain its relevancy for the new, developing situation?

In the book of Acts, Samaria becomes central to the mission: Jesus-followers will become "witnesses . . . in Jerusalem, in all Judea *and Samaria*, and to the ends of the earth" (Acts 1:8, my italics). Samaria's attachment to the key locations of Jerusalem and Judea is not incidental. The region was generally associated with the area of Judea (Acts 8:1). According to Acts, following the scattering of the disciples from Jerusalem due to Saul's persecution of the new movement, Philip brought the message of the coming Messiah to Samaria (8:5). Luke seems to intimate that even one notorious magician, Simon of Samaria, believed (8:9).[51] Luke then records that

---

48. See standard introductions. E.g., Powell, *Introducing the New Testament*, 161–81.

49. Cf. John 4 for another tradition about the origins of the gospel in Samaria. The Fourth Gospel includes female involvement in its origin story.

50. Pummer, *Samaritans*, 34.

51. Pummer does not think this Simon was a Samaritan (*Samaritans*, 36).

"Samaria had accepted the word of God" (8:14 NRSV). This claim parallels the tradition in John 4 but shifts the mission to Samaria to a later (post-Jesus) period. The lead apostles, Peter and John, followed up Philip's mission with one of their own, "proclaiming the good news to many villages of the Samaritans" (8:25 NRSV). Luke records a growing group of believers in Samaria (9:31) to the point that they were pleased to hear the report of gentile conversions from Paul and Barnabas (15:3). Nonetheless, the ears of "later" believers—from a time period in which many Samaritans were part of "the Way"—might have been deafened to the provocative nature of Jesus's Samaritan parable in its earlier context.[52]

Traditions Surrounding Samaritan Origins

Although these characterizations within early Christian and Jewish circles emphasize the *religious* difference of the Samaritans, do they also capture the *ethnic* difference of this group?[53] What are the origins of the Samaritans? Moreover, how were these traditions about origins remembered in the Judaism of Jesus's day? And how might they matter for Jesus's parable?

As a contemporary of Luke, the first-century Jewish historian Josephus provides significant insight into the multiple biblical traditions surrounding the origins of the Samaritans. His retelling of these traditions attests to the various ways Jewish people may have associated with their Samaritan neighbors during the period surrounding Luke's Gospel.

The oldest and most common tradition is found in 2 Kings 17.[54] This passage tells of the northern Assyrians' decisive defeat of the Israelites,

---

52. Bruce Longenecker makes a similar point in "Story of the Samaritan and the Innkeeper," 425–26.

53. Matthew Chalmers has recently called into question the two parts of the common reading of biblical scholarship—that is, the identification of the Samaritan as non-Jew and the characterization of the Samaritan as an enemy of first-century Jews (see "Rethinking Luke 10"). This article came to my attention too late in the process to incorporate more fully into this book.

54. Anderson, "Samaritans."

their southern neighbors. Part of Assyrian policy was to bring various people groups into the conquered land to intermingle among the remnants of the defeated. Perhaps marriages followed this interaction, but the narrative emphasizes the mixed religious worship experiment that had developed among the newcomers in Samaria, more so than any implied interethnic marriages: "So they worshiped the Lord [Yahweh] but also served their own gods" (2 Kings 17:41). The worship practice of this community was partially under the instruction of an Israelite priest who was sent back from exile to live among the people in Bethel.[55]

In his retelling of this account, Josephus downplays the arrival of multiple people groups and instead associates the Cutheans with the Samaritans in a much more direct way than 2 Kings. For Josephus, the Samaritans (or Cutheans) were immigrants to the land who treated the Israelites who remained in the land deceptively, considering them kinsfolk during prosperous times and treating them less kindly when it was beneficial to do so.[56] The Jewish historian's antagonism toward the Samaritans is quite explicit.

Another biblical tradition points to the rise of competing worship sites (Jerusalem and Mount Gerizim) following the return from Babylonian exile.[57] Ezra 4 reports a story of Israel's attempt to rebuild the temple in Jerusalem under the permission of the Persian king, Cyrus (v. 3). But their neighbors to the north, the Samaritans, were able to hinder this project with an appeal to a later king, insisting on the trouble the Israelites would make for the king if allowed to complete the rebuilding program. According to extrabiblical sources, both groups desired financial and political support from the Persians for the construction of separate central worship sites.[58] With political

---

55. According to Pummer, Luke does not hint at any link to 2 Kings 17 in his description of Samaritans (*Samaritans*, 36).

56. Josephus, *Ant.* 9.288–91.

57. Some scholars prefer to date Samaritan origins to the Persian period—from Cyrus's defeat of Babylon (539 BCE) to Alexander's defeat of the Persians (ca. 330 BCE)—partly because Jewish sources do not depict any Samaritans affected by the Babylonian exile; e.g., Cohen, *From the Maccabees to the Mishnah*, 162.

58. See the Elephantine papyri, cited by Anderson, "Samaritans," 76.

appeals of their own, Israel was able to complete their building project and celebrated its construction (Ezra 6).

According to Josephus, when the Samaritans offered to help, the Judean leadership refused their assistance; nonetheless, the Judeans invited them to worship there too.[59] This addition may be part of Josephus's rhetorical polemic since he did not report that the temple on Mount Gerizim was completed until a later period under Alexander the Great, although alternative Samaritan traditions trace the origins of Gerizim to the Persian era.[60]

Not all Jewish traditions describe a history in which the Samaritans and Jews are at odds with each other. During the latter half of the second century BCE, the author of 2 Maccabees (a Hellenistic Jew) detailed a period of high tension and revolutionary spirit under the violent and intrusive Seleucid king, Antiochus. From his perspective as one slightly more favorable to a Hellenistic environment, the author of 2 Maccabees considered Samaritans to be Jews, even though they worshiped at Gerizim and not in Jerusalem (e.g., 2 Macc. 5:22–23; 6:2).[61] Both places of worship came under attack from Antiochus's forces. The 2 Maccabees narrative provides no negative assessment of this alternative worship site.

Missing from the Maccabean literature, though present in Josephus's account, is the attack by John Hyrcanus, the Jewish high priest (134–104 BCE), of Mount Gerizim, primarily due to the Samaritans' acceptance of the Syrian king's policies.[62] In Josephus's report, the destruction of the Samaritan temple (on Gerizim) was viewed as the high priest's attempt to unify the country and to make every effort to enforce the Jewish manner of life on these surrounding territories— including Idumea.[63]

Earlier in the chapter I detailed Josephus's account of a more contemporary (to Josephus's, Jesus's, and Luke's day) incident of

59. Josephus, *Ant.* 11.84–87.
60. Josephus, *Ant.* 13.256–57; Anderson, "Samaritans," 76.
61. Also Pummer, *Samaritans*, 41.
62. Cohen, *From the Maccabees to the Mishnah*, 162.
63. Josephus, *Ant.* 13.254–58.

Jewish-Samaritan relationships that may have been more pertinent to the attitudes of his day, a case in which Claudius Caesar (r. 41–54 CE) intervened by appeal and sided with the Jewish people.[64] If Josephus was depicting the reality on the ground during the period a generation before he wrote, those tensions between Jews and Samaritans may have also been in the air a decade earlier (during Jesus's day).[65]

As we transition back to Luke's narrative context and work with Josephus's account of Jewish-Samaritan relations in or near Luke's period, we may be able to approximate the tension between the Jews and the Samaritans hinted at in the Gospel accounts. Against this backdrop, even John's Jesus exposes his Jewish bias with respect to the place of worship: "You worship what you do not know; we worship what we know, for salvation is from the Jews" (John 4:22 NRSV). This idea has a long tradition attached to it. Within Luke's narrative world, Samaritans are classified as "foreigners" (Luke 17:18), even if they are also considered Torah observers. This classification must have something to do with the difference in the site of their worship centers, if not also where they lived.[66]

It is possible that ethnic groups were classified in distinct ways in antiquity for characteristics other than those based on phenotype. Love Sechrest makes this argument in her research on the apostle Paul as "a former Jew."[67] She claims that religion (and the practice thereof) was key in distinguishing a person's ethnic group within ancient contexts. That is, a person was considered different ethnically if they worshiped differently.[68] Following Sechrest's categorization of "difference," perhaps religion was one way the ancients classified

---

64. Josephus, *J.W.* 2.232–49; *Ant.* 20.118–36.

65. Despite his wider thesis that Samaritans were part of Israel and should not be considered their enemies, Chalmers acknowledges the hostile portrayal of the Samaritans in Josephus's writings ("Rethinking Luke 10," 556). As a contemporary to the author of Luke, Josephus's tension-filled portrayal is key to the description here.

66. According to Pummer, the Samaritans belong to Israel for Luke, even though they did not attach significance to the temple in Jerusalem (*Samaritans*, 26).

67. Sechrest, *Former Jew*.

68. Is there a contemporary analogy in the way white Christians think about white Muslims, as something other than "white"?

ethnic difference. For Sechrest, "Because Jewish concepts of race and ethnicity placed religion at the center of identity instead of place of origin or kinship, Jewish identity had an elasticity not found in the other constructions of identity."[69] In any case, the stories circulating in Jewish tradition with respect to origins (see above) emphasize religious sites and practices and ethnic (or at least geographic) differences.[70]

The Lawyer's Response to the Parable (10:36–37)

The parable could have ended at verse 34, with the Samaritan bringing the injured person to an inn and taking care of him. Jesus could have ended with "they lived happily ever after" or said right then, "Go and do likewise." Instead, Jesus imagines a level of commitment partially consistent with the cultural mores of hospitality in his day while also expressing the deep commitment his imagined hero proffered. In addition to his immediate care, the Samaritan spent his time (he stayed the night), expended more of his resources ("took out two denarii"), and vowed to incur additional charges if necessary ("I will repay you whatever more you spend"). Subsequently, when Jesus turns back to the lawyer, the answer to his question should be obvious: "Which one of these three . . . was a neighbor?" (10:36 NRSV)

Many commentators observe that the lawyer (intentionally?) avoids the ethnic label of the do-gooder, referring to him simply as "the one who showed him mercy" (10:37).[71] This omission may have also encouraged later interpreters to downplay the ethnicity of the hero (e.g., Augustine). Much has been made of this avoidance, although Jesus did not react to it. The interlocutor's attention turns to the action of mercy. This term might be measured by how it is used in the wider narrative of Luke's Gospel. *Eleos* (mercy) is usually

---

69. Sechrest, *Former Jew*, 209.
70. Geographic location frequently stipulated a regional and ethnic difference among the ancients. Compare contemporary China, a country in which regional difference matters (e.g., Tibetans and Mongols).
71. E.g., Levine, "Luke," 137.

associated with God's attitude, memory, and response (1:50, 54, 58, 78) and is indicative of God's own commitment to the covenant God made with Israel (1:72). To act with mercy (i.e., to commit to the faithfulness of mercy toward others) is an act of the covenant (i.e., faithfully following Torah), and it is an act remembering God's own mercy. Nonetheless, Jesus's question alters the focus of the lawyer's initial probe as well, from "Who is my neighbor?" to "Which one was a neighbor?" From "To whom should I show mercy?" to "Who showed mercy?" From "Whom should I love?" to "Who showed love?" From the neighbor as the *object* of an action to the neighbor who functions as *subject* of the action.

My focus on the act of kindness may be an expression of my own type of Protestant Christian bias:[72] show me what you do when an injustice comes, and I'll tell you how that (in)action represents your faith. Amy-Jill Levine finds the emphasis on "doing" un-Jewish. It was part of the lawyer's test to ask a question that could not be answered: "One does not 'do' anything to inherit 'eternal life'" since Israel's election was a staple understanding of God's grace and was not dependent on works.[73] Levine's lawyer knows this; most first-century Jews would have known it as well. Jews followed Torah because it was God's gift, a sign of God's covenant with Israel. As any good Torah reader would know, "the Torah is not much interested in eternal life or life after death. It is much more interested in how to live in the present."[74] I agree. The Samaritan's act—from a Christian perspective—is not about whether the actor is a member of the covenant (whether God's salvation has reached them); it is about whether people are willing to extend God's salvation (the action of rescue and righteousness) to others. Furthermore, the Hebrew Bible (or Old Testament) as a whole is not much interested in eternal life

72. I must confess to my preference for the Wesleyan-leaning, Pelagian-informed Protestant type of Christian theology, rather than the Calvinistic-leaning, Augustinian-informed Protestant side of the Christian tradition.

73. Levine, *Short Stories by Jesus*, 85.

74. Levine, *Short Stories by Jesus*, 87.

or life after death either—or even in the resurrection of the dead.[75] Even eternal life is not about *doing*; living on earth, however, *is*. But the ethical life is also not simply about being and letting be. Bad things can happen to neighbors when we fail to act to support their just causes against the state's dehumanization of their very beings. Consequently, *doing* mercy may require much more from those who are committed to a theology of eternal life.

Jesus's final response to the lawyer rounds out the entire conversation: "Go and do likewise" (10:37). Although Luke describes an adversarial lawyer who confronts Jesus initially (v. 25) and desires to "justify" his own position (v. 29), here at the end of the account Luke does not describe the lawyer's reaction. Was he pleased with the outcome of his test? Did Jesus's parable about an act of mercy clarify for him what he came to seek? Or was his position so entrenched in a certain way of thinking that he was simply unable to hear the Jewish teacher? We can only speculate, and our speculation will reveal much more about us as interpreters than about the position or reaction of the characters in the narrative. Was the imaginative story enough to move him to action? Is it sufficient to move us?

Trauma and Future Commitments

It is possible to move past the trauma of a story too quickly. That is no less reflected in the scholarly attention on the Samaritan and the lawyer's final response ("The one who showed mercy"). The omission of the trauma is frequently driven by a common contemporary query summed up in the question "What is the point of the story?" But a story that moves beyond its author's intention, its narrative's context, and even its social setting may give impetus to new meaning possibilities and thereby become useful for further reflection

75. Only Isa. 26:19 and Dan. 12:2 seem to point to the theological idea of the general rising of dead bodies at the end of time. Jon Levenson suggests that there is more evidence within the Hebrew Bible in his *Resurrection and the Restoration of Israel*.

and probing new questions. The parable of Luke 10 offers those opportunities.

Not only does Jesus imagine a Samaritan as hero; he also imagines a tragedy. An unnamed man encounters robbers who leave him near death. How many hours does he lie on that hot, dusty road and reflect on his own death? As Stephanie Buckhanon Crowder reminds us, the Samaritan assisted a person who was a "victim of violence."[76] This man's wounds (Gk. *ta traumata*; 10:34) were serious enough that they required ongoing care, a commitment the Samaritan was apparently willing to make. Here might be the point at which many other advocates draw a line. It is one thing to participate in the initial action, to help someone in the immediacy of a traumatic crisis event. It is another matter to care for them for twenty-four hours (as the Samaritan did; see vv. 34–35). Furthermore, it is an additional matter altogether to commit to the kind of long-term care this abused man required. The Samaritan committed resources ("When I come back, I will repay you whatever more you spend") even though he did not (could not?) commit additional time at that moment. He, too, had other pressing matters. But the victim's trauma did not end with twenty-four-hour care. His body was not fully healed; his mind may not have yet been in the right place to continue his own journey. The immediate and necessary intervention was only the beginning of recovery. The story is open ended, with no sense of whether the man will ever return to full health; in fact, the opposite may be implied by the Samaritan's additional commitment: "Whatever is owed to you, I will repay it." Will the man ever fully recover? Will he recover his sight? The use of his legs? The use of his right hand? How damaging were the beatings (v. 30)? If he recovers fully physically, will he ever recover emotionally and psychologically? What may have been taken from him that he will never retrieve? Moreover, why should we pause at the ongoing trials of the victim? Jesus did not. Luke did not. Why should we?

76. Crowder, "Luke," 170.

Even though the Lukan narrative returns to the dialogue between Jesus and the lawyer (10:36–37) for resolution, the imagined victim of the parable and his ongoing health needs and well-being remain unexpressed. David Gowler recognizes that parables are "profoundly dialogic," since the resolution to parables "is continually granted to others."[77] For readers of the parable, why dwell on the trauma? *How do you read?* Jesus not only imagines a Samaritan as hero; he also imagines a tragic figure.

One of the Seventy

I was one of the seventy [Luke 10:1]. What a time we had in Sychar! My partner and I were the perfect odd couple. I could read and write, partly because my father was a scribe. My partner could do neither, but she had street smarts. She knew how to read people. She forewarned me about Sychar. She had a bad feeling about the place, but I asked, "If we don't bring the message to them, who will?" So she agreed, but only after some convincing. Looking back, I should have listened to my younger sister-partner (and future spouse).

We entered as "lambs into the midst of wolves" [10:3]. We simply (or, I should say, I simply) did not realize just how wolflike these folks would be. With minimal supplies, we were counting on the kindness of village people. You can find such people in most villages.

Thank God, that is our culture. I hear of some foreign cities in which beggars remain in the squalor of the streets for weeks and months without anyone noticing them.

This village, however, was unlike any we had experienced in the past several days. After the eighth or ninth house (I lost count), and realizing that we would have to remain near the village gates for the night and wait for daylight to travel to the next village, we finally went into the town square near the main market of the village. Sarai said at the top of

77. Gowler, *What Are They Saying*, 103.

her lungs, "Even the dust of your town that clings to our feet, we wipe off in protest against you. Yet know this: the kingdom of God has come near" [10:11].

When we left early the next morning, we noticed a small group of men watching us intently. We didn't realize until later that they followed us.

It was a full, positive, eventful day as we entered two small, adjacent villages that welcomed us with open arms. They provided lots of good food—bread, cheese, fish, fried sardines, and anchovies—and we wanted to spend a night or two. But the seventy had planned to gather with Jesus late that evening, so we needed to be on our way.

After the joyous celebration with Jesus, hearing all of the excitement from so many of our peers, we, too, shared the good news about our experiences during the past few days.

When everyone was going their separate ways to find times of rest and to check back in on families, Sarai and I also said farewell to each other. We agreed that we would meet up again in a week to touch base with Jesus and the group and see what new direction we might participate in. Even in our final goodbyes, we still had not realized that someone was following us.

Then it all happened in a blur . . .

I have been thinking a lot lately about Jesus's promise of protection that nothing would hurt us [10:19]. Initially, I got really angry about the brutal beating I received. How much authority does Jesus have if he's unable to keep us safe when we are on specific missions for him? How could his God have let me down?

Then I catch myself: Am I asking the wrong questions? I realize that my head is not yet clear enough to process what I think about all that has happened. I remember that my life has been spared; I have received mercy.

These are some of my thoughts as I slowly recover under the care of the innkeeper, whose kindness I have come to cherish. What I did not know until the third day was that it was a Samaritan who saved me and brought me to this inn—a *Samaritan*. When they relayed that part of the story to me, they also told me it would be a couple more days before the Samaritan returned.

I had received mercy from a *Samaritan*!

The Trauma beyond the Parable

A traumatic event has a way of shaping the memory of the traumatized for many years to come.[78] It may cause some to rethink everything they hold dear, including the way a person thinks about their faith, their understanding of God's actions in the world. Trauma may also affect human relationships, especially if the harm originates from someone the person knows and from whom they expect love. Trauma theorists point out that previous experience of trauma may also negatively impact potentially painful events in the future. Communal support becomes crucial for assisting traumatized people who remain on the healing journey. Since the disturbing event never fully leaves the mind, it is a journey! Returning to the parable story, the amount of trauma the victim in the story faced as a child might determine how well he would recover from this latest event.

Furthermore, trauma may have wide-ranging consequences on people other than the original victim. Some cultures (and families) may be better situated to care for traumatized people in their midst. The level of commitment the parable calls for moves beyond the Samaritan's own; it calls for a communal commitment. While the innkeeper might be repaid for his ongoing care for the victim, other areas of his business might suffer.[79] Would the leaky roof get fixed? Would he be unable to secure necessary goods from the neighboring town during this time? If he was still able to maintain his business while caring for the victim, hospitality would require the assistance of his family, his wife's (or their slaves') cooking, his children (or their slaves) running errands, and so on. Perhaps the ancient Mediterranean cultural setting was more accustomed to providing this kind of human care, without counting the immediate economic costs, than is our contemporary one.[80] Jesus's story may end with his query (Which

78. Bloom, "Trauma Theory Abbreviated."
79. For Augustine's more meaningful role for the innkeeper through the allegorical method, see chap. 2 above.
80. Ancient people calculated economic costs when time allowed, since it would be shameful not to do so: "If one of you wanted to build a tower, wouldn't you first

one of these *three*?), yet it provokes the imagination to count the continuing costs of money, time, and social capital that all true traumas require. Where is the ancient clinical psychologist who will give of her time and resources to assist this victim back to "full" health?

As the story goes, the innkeeper will have to function as the short-term ancient clinician—that is, as the one, along with his family, who will have to deal with the initial aspects of the trauma.[81] In biblical literature, the Greek word *pandocheus* occurs only here. Its meaning as "one who welcomes all" might be attractive to the Lukan ecclesial community.[82] In a recent scholarly article, Bruce Longenecker argues for the crucial role of this usually overlooked minor character.[83] First, he attempts to show that in ancient culture folks in Jesus's audience would consider these hosts "morally dubious figures."[84] This debatable cultural assumption—unclear from a straightforward reading of the parable in Luke 10 and the absence of such characters from the remainder of the Lukan narrative—is crucial for Longenecker's argument that Jesus's listeners would have expected a different response from the innkeeper, perhaps even a refusal of the Samaritan's request. Whatever one might think of the innkeeper's action in Luke's brief description, I agree with Longenecker that a mutual trust must have occurred on the necessary expenses in order to restore the victim back to full health.[85] For Longenecker, the innkeeper's actions are as crucial to the man's recovery as the Samaritan's, since many activities could have hindered the latter from returning to the inn.[86]

---

sit down and calculate the cost, to determine whether you have enough money to complete it? Otherwise, when you have laid the foundation but couldn't finish the tower, all who see it will begin to belittle you. They will say, 'Here's the person who began construction and couldn't complete it!'" (Luke 14:28–30 CEB).

81. John Chrysostom substitutes a "trained physician" for the innkeeper in his retelling of the story. Quoted in Longenecker, "Story of the Samaritan and the Innkeeper," 429.

82. The word did not occur in the writings of Philo or Josephus (BDAG, 753).

83. Longenecker, "Story of the Samaritan and the Innkeeper."

84. Longenecker, "Story of the Samaritan and the Innkeeper," 432.

85. Longenecker, "Story of the Samaritan and the Innkeeper," 440.

86. Longenecker, "Story of the Samaritan and the Innkeeper," 441–42.

Should this story be called the "Compassionate Samaritan and the Trustworthy Innkeeper"? That would have been a twist for Jesus's original audience.

Might these types of trauma stories help us understand the Lukan community? Did they prepare Luke's readers for the physical and mental abuses followers of Jesus were facing? Did these trauma events hint at the possibility that assistance may come from unexpected places—for example, from people of different ethnic backgrounds or religious persuasions (e.g., Samaritans) or from potentially, typically untrustworthy individuals (e.g., innkeepers)?

With Whom Should Readers Identify?

Many interpreters recognize that a first-century Jewish audience would have expected a Jewish teacher to tell a story in which the three characters of comparison were a priest, a Levite, and a common Jew.[87] A straightforward account would have assumed these three characters were representatives of different segments from within Jewish society. The audience would have also assumed that the victim was a Jew. The primary point of the story, in this case, would have been that all Jews need to be responsible Torah-obeying Jews; Jews in official positions hold no advantage over the common Jew. All are responsible to God and to one another.

Imagine if Jesus had told the story in this way, but the victim was a Samaritan—if a Jew had rescued a Samaritan victim. What would Jesus's Jewish audience have thought then?[88] It might have been similar to the story of Jonah in Jewish tradition. At one point Luke depicts just this kind of action in Jesus's life, albeit not in parable form: at the request of his Jewish elders Jesus heals a person enslaved to a Roman centurion (7:1–10). A Jew assisting a non-Jew has precedent and would highlight Torah as well (see Lev.

87. Levine, *Short Stories by Jesus*, 103.
88. The story may recall 2 Chron. 28, in which enemy Samaritans assist Jewish captives.

19:33–34).[89] This alternative may have been what Harriet Jacobs had in mind with her wounded Samaritan (see chap. 2). For her, should not a Southern white person (think Jew) help an enslaved black individual in dire need of assistance (think wounded Samaritan)? Perhaps, in the racialized context of the nineteenth century, the association of "white" with "Jew"—an irony in the nineteenth century in many places—forced her to think in these terms.[90]

Jesus, however, reverses the audience's expectation: a Samaritan becomes the savior of the Jew. Although the ethnic identity of the victim is not specifically identified, the lack of an identifying marker suggests (to this reader) that the character is Jewish.[91] In Luke's narrative world non-Jews are usually identified (7:2);[92] Jews need not be acknowledged as such within a Jewish story. People in Jesus's audience would have readily identified with the victim;[93] this association would be much less likely if the victim were a non-Jew.

Levine argues that Jesus's audience would identify with the victim.[94] Levine insists, rightfully, on interpreting Jesus's parables in ways that forgo anti-Semitic positions, which are often perpetrated

89. The Jewish elders made this request because this non-Jew, who had a good working relationship with the local Jewish community, provided financial support for the construction of the synagogue (Luke 7:4–5).

90. The situation, of course, is more complicated than that simple equation. There are many instances in which Jacobs also associated enslaved blacks (and other people of African descent) with biblical Israel. See Powery, "'Rise Up, Ye Women,'" 171–84.

91. A few scholars think the ethnic identity of the victim is less clear. Luise Schottroff does not think ethnicity is crucial here, since the text "does *not* say that the victim is a Jew, so that the Samaritan's love overcomes a barrier" (*Parables of Jesus*, 134). Jesus did not, however, have to provide the expected ethnic label. Most of the characters in his parables were, unsurprisingly, Jews. In light of this discussion, we should also (re)consider the ethnic identity of the robbers, with which few interpreters trouble themselves. Perhaps contemporary readers in capitalistic environments ought to identify with the robbers in this account.

92. In addition to the Samaritans of Luke 10 and Luke 17, note also the gentile centurion of Luke 7.

93. Levine, *Short Stories by Jesus*, 94–95. Would the lack of a clear identity marker also have allowed Luke's gentile readers to locate themselves in the victim?

94. This identification would also be true for later readers of the story according to Robert Funk (quoted in Gowler, *What Are They Saying*, 21). Also Nolland, *Luke 9:21–18:34*, 592. Another interpretive tradition may be traced to Augustine, according

(unknowingly at times) by many Christian-leaning interpreters. There are at least three helpful reminders from Levine to consider as we continue to reflect theologically on this parable. First, identification with parable characters is a common experience for readers of the parables. Levine asserts that most later readers identify with the Samaritan, and the problem with this identification is that it "leads to the standard anti-Jewish interpretations that have infected much of New Testament study."[95] Second, she observes, rightly, that this is not a story about "impurity," as if purity concerns explain the actions of the priest and Levite. The narrative level seems to support this idea; that is, the priest and Levite are *departing* from Jerusalem and would have been less concerned about purity *after* their service at the Jerusalem temple.[96] In addition, as Levine recognizes, "There is nothing impure about touching a person who is 'half dead.'"[97] Finally, when Levine turns her attention to the Samaritan character, she beckons interpreters to view the Samaritan "as did its original audience," as an enemy and not as one who was oppressed.[98] Other scholars have also noted that the key to the story is to place the "hated Samaritan" at the heart of the story.[99] Jewish listeners who might have associated with the victim might have thought, in Levine's words, "I'd rather die than acknowledge that one from that group saved me."[100]

to whom readers should identify with the victim, since Augustine's Christ figure is represented, allegorically, by the Samaritan.

95. Levine, *Short Stories by Jesus*, 80.

96. Luke 10:31 implies that the priest was traveling in the same direction as the wounded man: from Jerusalem to Jericho. Jews in the Second Temple period were less concerned about purity laws as they distanced themselves from the temple precincts. See Cohen, *From the Maccabees to the Mishnah*, 124–25.

97. Levine, *Short Stories by Jesus*, 100. For many interpreters, implied purity concerns are at stake. Jesus's parable, however, draws attention to the inaction of the priest and Levite, not to the cause of their inaction (also Nolland, *Luke 9:21–18:34*, 593–94). For a Lukan story in which Jesus explicitly challenges the purity concerns of the Pharisees, see Luke 11:37–54.

98. Levine, *Short Stories by Jesus*, 104.

99. See Gowler, *What Are They Saying*, 9. Although Chalmers acknowledges the presence of the "tension" motif in some of the ancient sources (e.g., Josephus), he argues that the enemy motif is not the best option ("Rethinking Luke 10," 565).

100. Levine, *Short Stories by Jesus*, 104.

Luke's Ethnic Ideology and the Samaritan

Levine discovers diverse views within the rabbinic sources; some rabbis considered Samaritans similar to Jews, and others did not.[101] In the time of Jesus, however, the "enemy" label seems to be key for wrestling with the parable. Levine does not make much of the ethnic label, except to acknowledge how Jesus's Jewish audience would have reacted. In fact, she ends this section with a warning: "Readers will need to determine if the end, the passionate call for liberation, justifies the means, if the means turn out to be a negative caricature of Jewish culture."[102] With attention to her contemporary audience, this is one of Levine's primary concerns. One needs only to look at recent incidents in contemporary society, including the 2018 deadly shooting inside a Pittsburgh synagogue in which eleven people were killed and many others were injured. Nonetheless, from the perspective of modern nonwhite readers, the ethnic identity of the Samaritan (and his status in relationship to ancient Judaism) matters deeply.

Cain Hope Felder agrees but notes that readers should not simply identify with the Samaritan without a critical examination of Luke's ideological tendencies.[103] In Felder's description, Luke's ethnic tendency was to relay a story that is constantly moving westward, a story that shifts the development of the early Christian community from Jerusalem to Rome. This story line should not be accepted at face value historically, however, since Luke's storytelling agenda was not innocent. These geographical indicators were not neutral sites, ideologically speaking. The narrator had an agenda that shifts the overarching message of Jesus from the "narrow" confines of Jerusalem to the Latinized, "expansive" world of the West. The story

101. Levine, *Short Stories by Jesus*, 109. Cf. Schiffman, "Samaritans in Tannaitic Halakhah," 333.

102. Levine, *Short Stories by Jesus*, 110–11.

103. This critical lens stems from a black hermeneutic, as Itumeleng Mosala suggests, "A hermeneutical category of black theology would begin a reading of Luke's discourse by drawing daggers against his ideological intentions. It would refuse to be drawn into an appreciation of an 'orderly' presentation of Jesus and his movement" (*Biblical Hermeneutics and Black Theology*, 175).

of the early church does not take its readers to the Eastern regions with its "browner" populations, or to the Southern countries with its "blacker" populations. For Felder, Luke's artistic agenda was to portray the development of Christianity through a "whitening" of the believing community, away from its Indigenous lands and peoples, a move that has forever altered the conversation about Christian origins. For Felder, Luke's ideological tendency to tell the westward story was shared by others within the New Testament collection that was organized years later: "The immediate significance of this New Testament tendency to focus on Rome instead of Jerusalem is that the darker races outside the Roman orbit are for the most part overlooked by New Testament authors."[104] Luke was not telling an impartial story of the development of early Christian growth; Luke presented a story in order to shape his present. Felder acknowledges Luke's overall objective in this portrayal, while still recognizing the ambiguity of the Lukan narrative.[105] This Lukan ambivalence leads to Felder's assessment: "This by no means suggests that Luke had a negative attitude about Black people."[106] Despite his general direction, Luke articulates a racial pluralism in the description of the leadership of the church in Antioch (Acts 13:1).

Felder opens up a world of possibility for digging more deeply into Luke's theology of the "other"—that is, Luke's ideological depiction of ethnic groups. How does Luke construct the other? What might Luke offer for reflection on ethnic difference? To what extent does Rome stand over against Jerusalem in Luke's narrative world, if not

104. Felder, *Troubling Biblical Waters*, 46. The Gospel of Mark does not escape Felder's criticism: "It is no coincidence that Mark . . . goes to such great lengths to show that the confession of the Roman centurion brings his whole gospel narrative to its climax" (p. 46).

105. Furthermore, for Felder, Luke's portrait results in "a circumstantial de-emphasis of a Nubian (African) in favor of an Italian (European) and thereby enables some Europeans to claim or imply that Acts demonstrates some divine preference for Europeans" (*Troubling Biblical Waters*, 48). According to Margaret Aymer, the Ethiopian was likely a "multilingual Jew able to interface easily with empire" ("Acts of the Apostles," 541).

106. Felder, *Troubling Biblical Waters*, 47.

also in Luke's lived experience? Finally, for our purposes, how might a *Samaritan* fit within any of these narrative portrayals of difference?

Whether one agrees with Felder's thesis is less important than recognizing that Luke's ethnic lens is worth investigating—if ever so briefly in a project like this one—especially for a story like the parable under exploration. In fact, it is the only parable in which Jesus centralizes a non-Jewish figure. What difference does a merciful Samaritan make within Luke's larger geopolitical and socioethnic parameters? Alternatively, if the historical Jesus had little contact with the Samaritans—as the earliest Gospel, Mark, depicts and many historians conclude[107]—what would have been Luke's ideological or theological agenda for placing a Samaritan at the heart of Jesus's parable? As Toni Morrison reminds us, reflecting on the writing of racial constructions in American literature, the identification of an outsider is often an attempt to define the self: "Literature is especially and obviously revelatory in exposing/contemplating the definition of self whether it condemns or supports the means by which it is acquired."[108] So what was Luke up to? Moreover, how does he envision his developing Christian community in light of the Samaritan parable?

What Has Rome to Do with a Samaritan?

Rome is the epicenter of Luke's world and, thereby, a primary target for the new religious movement. Luke tells his story with Rome as the narrative framework. From the emperor's decree (Luke 2:1) to Paul's unhindered preaching in Rome (Acts 28:30–31), Luke's story shifts the interests and events from Jerusalem to the "ends of the earth" within his narrative framework (Acts 1:8). Overall, as Margaret Aymer ob-

---

107. Moreover, the Samaritan village's refusal to host Jesus and his traveling party (Luke 9) maintains this Synoptic Gospel "history," which, of course, is challenged by the Fourth Gospel (John 4).

108. Morrison, *Origin of Others*, 6. This publication is based on a series of talks Morrison gave at Harvard in 2016 on "the literature of belonging."

serves, Luke presents a "more conciliatory stance toward the Roman occupation."[109] Throughout the two-part work, Luke offers several portrayals of positive contacts between Jews and Romans. Even Jesus, at the behest of some Jewish elders, heals a Roman centurion's slave (Luke 7). Luke complicates the relationship between Rome and Jerusalem when he, apparently, places the bulk of the blame for Jesus's death on the leaders from the latter group.[110] Among the Gospels, only Luke depicts an intricate networking of political forces at work surrounding Jesus's trial. The coordination between the Roman Pilate and the Jewish Herod—and the innocence each one announced in the case of Jesus—led Luke to depict a special bond between the two leaders: "That same day Herod and Pilate became friends with each other" (Luke 23:12 NRSV). The Jerusalem leaders, however, receive the brunt of the blame for Jesus's death in Luke's account (23:23). Besides, this charge will continue into the sequel as the story of Acts relentlessly reminds the audience of those responsible for Jesus's death (Acts 2:22–23; 3:13–15; 4:10; 5:30). The tendency to shift this blame, as Itumeleng Mosala recognizes, fails to account for the significance of a death "in the face of the repressive and murderous state machinery of 'law and order.'"[111] Whatever role the Jerusalem leadership played in this execution, only Rome and its representatives could legally carry out this capital punishment. However innocent in Luke's description, Pilate must have given the ultimate order for this execution. So Luke's less than straightforward (historical?) account of the death of Jesus reveals much more about Luke's tendency to appeal to Rome, in order to encourage a peaceful Roman future for the developing movement of Jesus, than it reveals the facts on the ground. If this narrative tendency is about power, then for the sake of the survival of the small, fledgling movement, Luke attempts to inform those in power that Christianity is no threat to Rome. If this narrative tendency is about ethnic identity, then Luke's preference

109. Aymer, "Acts of the Apostles," 536.
110. Also Mosala, *Biblical Hermeneutics and Black Theology*, 178.
111. Mosala, *Biblical Hermeneutics and Black Theology*, 175.

for the westward expansion of the movement typifies a focus on the Latinized segments of the Christian movement. Political power or ethnic identity? Can the two be fully separate from each other?

Before we turn our attention back to the Samaritan of the parable, a short review of Acts for additional information on Luke's tendencies within the narrative's ethnic ideology would be helpful.

The Story of Acts Depicts a World of Ethnic Difference and Ethnic Unity

Attuned to the impact of migration and ethnic identity in contemporary politics, some scholars recognize the significance of "movement" and of "people groups" within the two-part story of Luke-Acts. Those interpreters who ignore the ethnic dimensions of Scripture—both ethnic characters and ethnic ideology—reveal more about themselves as interpreters than about the ancient world. Some of these interpreters assume (or claim or desire) to live in a "color-blind" society, so they impose—sometimes unwittingly—the same on the ancient communities, especially on their "Christian" predecessors. If nothing else, the Bible is full of tales about ethnic groups, conflicts, and migrations. One key opening story in Acts is the story of Pentecost, in which we find multiple languages being spoken and Jews "from every nation" present (Acts 2). Nevertheless, grasping Luke's theology of the other has not generated a consensus. For Eric Barreto, the narrative of Luke-Acts values difference: "Difference is a gift from God to the world according to Acts."[112] For others, such as Benny Liew, "Acts has an ethnicity problem."[113]

For Barreto, a discussion about Luke-Acts' view of "difference" should be understood in light of how one interprets this narrative's relationship to empire. He interprets Acts as an anti-imperial force, since Rome is a "force of imperial power [that desires] to impose

112. Barreto, "Whence Migration?," 137.
113. Liew, "Acts," 422.

cultural homogeneity."[114] Most scholars would agree on this view of empire but not necessarily on the stance Luke takes.[115] On the other hand, Luke counters this hegemony—for Barreto—by extending "a theological vision" that upholds the importance of ethnic difference. Furthermore, Barreto concludes, "The Holy Spirit empowers the formation of a radical community of inclusivity that invites and nurtures ethnic diversity."[116] It is an interpretation and vision I gladly accept, but it is unclear that *Luke* promotes it unambiguously.

Liew, on the other hand, acknowledges this ambivalence. Despite the presence of gentiles—Nicolaus of Antioch (Acts 6:5), the Ethiopian eunuch (8:26–40), and Cornelius (chap. 10)—as key figures in the developing but still mostly Jewish Christian community, Luke's "ethnicity problem," for Liew, stems from Luke's reluctance to report an account of "any non-Jewish missionary."[117] Instead, Luke depicts only Jewish missionary activity, though some were Aramaic-speaking believers while others were Greek-speaking believers (Acts 6). However, even though Luke never presents gentile believers participating in any event in which they take the message to other communities (or even to their own), Luke provides portrayals, albeit brief, of ethnoracially diverse Jewish believers (ethnically diverse from Judean believers) who took the central message of the movement elsewhere (Acts 11:20, 26). Luke offers a more ethnically diverse Jewish group of believers than what some contemporary interpreters may envision.

Liew rightfully acknowledges the complexities of distinguishing "race" from "ethnicity" in ancient sources, even though there are occasional hints that those sources may have done so in some cases

114. Barreto, "Whence Migration?," 143.

115. Following the majority of scholarship on Acts, Aymer suggests that Luke offers a "more conciliatory stance toward Roman occupation" ("Acts of the Apostles," 536).

116. Barreto, "Whence Migration?," 144.

117. Liew, "Acts," 422. But, alas, Luke did not do so. Most scholars argue that the eunuch was a gentile "God-fearer" (and not Jewish) in light of the prescription in Deut. 23:1.

(e.g., Acts 21:38, when Paul is misidentified as an unnamed Egyptian). Reflecting on Acts 2:5–11, Cynthia Baker reminds us that Luke chose the "Jews as the template for imagining unity suffusing an otherwise incoherent babble of ethnic distinction and diversity. . . . The ethnoracial diversity of the Jews persists and is emphasized in the account."[118] For Luke, then, the Jews become the "*model*—not merely his *foil* or *counterpoint*—for imagining a universal, multiethnic, spirit-filled community."[119] It is crucial to avoid the mistakes of past interpreters who assumed that "Jew" meant a "particular" identity and "Christian" meant a "universal" identity and that a distinction between the two "groups" made all the difference in the world. That is not the story Luke-Acts communicates.

Even though non-Jewish missionary activity is absent from the narrative, Luke depicted interethnic marriages without comment. A Roman governor Felix was married to a Jew, Drusilla (Acts 24:24). Timothy's mother was a Jewish Christ-follower; his father was a Greek (16:1). The latter case deserves further discussion and may be viewed on various levels. Aymer reflects on it from Timothy's perspective, as one for whom it "is a political act of 'choosing sides' between his Greek father and his Jewish mother."[120] Luke's Paul—a Paul who should be compared carefully and critically to the Paul of the letters—had Timothy circumcised so that he could participate in the Pauline mission among Jews (16:3). The Paul of Acts chooses sides. Similar to Luke's Jesus, Luke's Paul remains Jewish to the core. His own defense in Rome is explicit: "I have in no way committed an offense against the law of the Jews, or against the temple, or against the emperor" (25:8 NRSV). According to Barreto, Timothy's "mixed" identity, for Luke, "represents the joining of Jew and Greek that does not obliterate ethnic difference."[121] Although the ethnicity

118. Baker, "From Every Nation under Heaven," 92.
119. Baker, "From Every Nation under Heaven," 95 (her italics).
120. Aymer, "Acts of the Apostles," 542.
121. Barreto, "Whence Migration?," 142. This idea is more ambivalent in the Acts narrative. Coming from one single speech, Paul apparently emphasizes the oblitera-

of first-century children was determined patrilineally, the "gentile" side of Timothy's interethnic lineage—in Liew's argument—must be subsumed under his Jewish identity in order to carry out the (Lukan-Pauline) mission in Acts.[122] Whatever one thinks about Acts 16:1–3, it falls oddly on the heels of a decision by James and other prominent leaders of the new movement *not* to circumcise gentiles who had become believers (Acts 15). Apparently, following Luke's narrative, there is one ecclesial decision for gentiles *after they have entered the fold* and a separate decision for interethnic gentiles to be able to participate in the Lukan-Jewish Pauline mission.

When we turn to the Lukan origin story for the gospel reaching the Samaritans (Acts 8:4–25; cf. John 4), we see that it was Philip, one of the seven Greek-speaking Jewish believers, who proclaimed the message there, linking the Samaritans in Luke's narrative construction with the Greek-speaking (and not Aramaic-speaking) side of the map. As the story unfolds, Philip's message needs confirmation from headquarters (i.e., the Jerusalem apostles) who send Peter and John to sanction the event (why else would they have come?) and grant the Samaritan community the more complete message since, as a narrative sidenote indicates, "as yet the Spirit had not come upon any of them; they had only been baptized in the name of the Lord Jesus" (Acts 8:16 NRSV). This seems to have less to do with the ethnic identity of the Samaritan group than with Luke's emphasis on the central authority of the Jerusalem leadership. Luke reports a parallel event in Acts 18:24–19:7—another account in which faith in Christ without possession of the Spirit is depicted as inferior—but this time among Jews in Ephesus.[123] Liew's analogy to contemporary

---

tion of ethnic difference ("From one ancestor he made all nations to inhabit the whole earth") and the preservation of geographical difference (God also "allotted the times of their existence and the boundaries of the places where they would live"; Acts 17:26 NRSV). Demetrius Williams provides a brief history on the African American use of Acts 17:26 as a fundamental idea in the development of the "one blood doctrine," which was crucial in the fight for racial equality ("Acts of the Apostles," 236–38).

122. Compare this story to the one about "Titus" in Gal. 2, in Paul's own words.

123. Liew describes these two accounts as stories highlighting an "inferior faith," until the Spirit is fully granted ("Acts," 420).

immigration is worth repeating: "If faith in Christ is like obtaining a 'green card' that grants entry and residency, the coming of the Holy Spirit is comparable to the 'naturalization' process that (theoretically) turns a 'green-card' holder into a citizen eligible for equal rights and benefits."[124] At least Luke's two-tiered system of entry into the Way did not seem to include (on the surface) an ethnic bias.

In the final analysis, does Luke-Acts have an ethnicity problem, or is the two-part narrative portrayal of the growth of the early church a model for the gift of diversity? Our response may depend less on the story's words than on our presuppositions about the meaning and value of difference. Even Felder's broad thesis on Luke's ethnic focus on the geographical journey of the community may find problematic elements in, on the one hand, Luke's allusions to subtle corruptions among the Roman representatives (Acts 24:26–27; 25:9) and, on the other hand, Luke's emphasis on the ethnic diversity of the Jews. Not all is well with Rome—and its diplomats![125] While Luke's narrative imagines a "world of ethnoracial diversity among the Jews"[126] as well as the involvement of other ethnic groups in the movement, it is not always easy to discern the implicit narrative bias. There is ambiguity and ambivalence on several fronts.[127] Yet it is worthwhile to acknowledge some of these tensions because it forces many contemporary readers not to ignore the ethnic and linguistic elements of the Lukan narrative. It is a story about ethnic groups, diversity, and conflict. It is a story in which Luke gives preference to some groups over others. With respect to ethnic difference, this ancient biblical account may

124. Liew, "Acts," 421.

125. Also Liew, "Acts," 426.

126. Baker, "From Every Nation under Heaven," 95.

127. There are challenges on several fronts. With respect to Luke's portrayal of female characters, Jane Schaberg and Sharon Ringe recognize the following: "But enthusiasm for Luke-Acts, the most massive work in the New Testament, is enthusiasm for a formidable opponent, not for an ally" ("Gospel of Luke," 511). In the same commentary collection, Aymer reacts to the unwillingness of Luke to allow for pluralism: Acts "is the source of theological and ethical assertions that have been central within movements of justice, while stigmatizing entire groups of holy people who believe differently from The Way" ("Acts of the Apostles," 538).

open up avenues of possibility for contemporary conversations. But the conclusions of Luke-Acts—Luke's bias specifically—may not always lead the way forward.

What difference does this brief analysis make for our understanding of Jesus's parable? Before we return to the parable, there is still one more (in)directly related passage we need to pursue to understand Luke's view. In Luke 17, Jesus labels the gracious Samaritan—who returned to give thanks for his healing—a "foreigner" (Gk. *allogenēs*; v. 18 NRSV). The Greek term *allogenēs* occurs once in the New Testament collection but was a synonym for *allophylos* (foreigner) in Peter's description of Cornelius in the other Lukan narrative (Acts 10:28). *Allogenēs* would also have reminded first-century readers of the well-known inscription located at the Jerusalem temple site: "No *foreigner* should enter here."[128]

Despite its rare usage, *allogenēs* was a loaded word. Barreto suggests that Jesus's statement—"Has no one returned to give praise to God *except this foreigner?*"—had a significant tone, "an edge of condemnation and dismissal."[129] The term occasionally carried censuring overtones in other Jewish-Greek literature of the period (cf. Jdt. 9:2; Sir. 45:13), including language linked to the coming age of the Messiah, when God would no longer allow the "foreigner" to live among the Jews (Pss. Sol. 17:28). Perhaps it carried this sharpness even for Luke's Jesus, especially if the rejection of the Samaritan village (Luke 9:51–56) was still fresh in his mind. In any case, Jesus expresses the sentiment as a surprising challenge to his Jewish compatriots. To put it colloquially, "Even a Samaritan knows how to be grateful! Should 'we' not know better?" An obvious tone surfaces in the sentiment.

Whatever else the Luke 17 story might conjure up, the account also implies that the Jews and the Samaritans shared some theological practices (since Jesus also sent the Samaritan to the priests for confirmation). Presumably, since their ethnicity is unstated, the other

128. BDAG, 46.
129. Barreto, "Except This Foreigner?"

unnamed people all formerly touched by leprosy were Jews. Here, some scholars prefer to focus on the difference between Samaritan and Jew. Levine suggests that the healed Samaritan leper would have to go to the priests at Mount Gerizim to carry out Jesus's instructions.[130] Even if that were the case, the narrative focuses less on this difference in worship sites and more on the implied camaraderie among those affected by the disease and, eventually, on the individual who returned. On this final point—the one who returned—*difference*, then, is emphasized, presumably as a critique of Jesus's own community: "Even a Samaritan knows how to be grateful!" The lawyer apparently captures this critique when he acknowledges (without mention of the ethnic label): "the one who showed him mercy" (Luke 10:37). On the other hand, Luke's increasingly gentile community of Christ-followers, who preserved this story, may have reacted with anti-Semitic overtones. What do you hear? How do you read?

As David Gowler reminds us, "every interpretation 'modernizes Jesus.'"[131] Each of the later representatives—Augustine, Jacobs, Thurman, the Solentiname community—could be said to be interpreters operating in a context of trauma. For Augustine, the Donatist conflict caused many Catholic Christians to respond to their neighbors in disruptive ways. Empowered by the support of the emperor, Augustine himself advocated for the use of violence, if necessary, in light of his reading of Luke 14:23 ("compel people to come in").[132] The traumatic contexts of others (from chap. 2) are more easily discernible. Harriet Jacobs penned her story in the antebellum period and published it on the eve of the US Civil War. She worked through some of her trauma in the writing and retelling of her story (and the writing of letters) but waited for her grandmother's death before pub-

130. Levine, "Luke," 151.
131. Gowler, *What Are They Saying*, 73.
132. Cooper, *Augustine for Armchair Theologians*, 197.

licly acknowledging this account. Howard Thurman was a nationally known minister living and preaching throughout segregated America. Up until Thurman's *Jesus and the Disinherited*, Thurman's America did not look much different from Jacobs's postwar America in terms of racial trauma. In the midst of their nation's trauma, the Solentiname community gathered and wrestled with the biblical stories of their faith in an attempt to imagine a better world and their role in it. If the story of Acts is a guide, ongoing struggles among the early Christ-followers in Luke's context may have included ethnic conflict, religious tension, and family separations, even while these followers attempted to portray a unified developing Christian movement that was, on the one hand, hoping to present itself in less tension with the Roman Empire while, on the other hand, emphasizing its separation from the Judaism from which its leading adherents came. Within this context, Luke's Jesus tells the parable about an unassuming Samaritan who shows mercy.

We now turn to the final chapter to discuss the theological possibilities this story may offer to the contemporary church.

4

Samaritan Lives Matter

Is the Church Engaged in Good Trouble?

I began writing this final chapter during a global pandemic. During the early months of summer 2020, it was hard to imagine the toll this pandemic would take on the world. By the time this volume is publicly available, COVID-19 may no longer be the threat that it was in 2020–2021. The science community has made significant progress to develop vaccines that can at least curb the virus's most deadly effects. Yet at the time of this writing, the death toll is over 620,000 in the US and over 4.3 million worldwide.[1]

I also began this chapter during another "pandemic."[2] It is one we have previously witnessed and, sadly, this "virus" will return. This new "outbreak" has been defined by a number, 9:29, a number that refers to the amount of time a police officer (Officer Derek Chauvin) held his knee on the neck of a forty-six-year-old African American man named George Floyd—nine minutes and twenty-nine seconds.

1. See "COVID Data Tracker," Centers for Disease Control and Prevention, accessed August 26, 2021, https://covid.cdc.gov/covid-data-tracker/#datatracker-home.
2. Many have acknowledged as much. In biblical studies, see recently Hidalgo, "Scripturalizing the Pandemic," 625–34.

Before you proceed, I encourage you to pause, set your stopwatch on your cellphone, and pray for nine minutes and twenty-nine seconds to sense just how long that time frame is.

In the parable before us there are at least four lives that matter, each of which represents others. As a sidenote, because of the patriarchal context of the biblical texts, we should not be surprised that all four lives in this text are male. Within the Gospel of Luke, the story that follows—an account about two sisters (Mary and Martha)—should be read in conjunction with this parable as a possible way this ancient writer attempted to balance the patriarchal systems in place: by counterbalancing male-centered stories with other accounts in which females play key character roles.

In the case of Luke 10, the four representatives are the unnamed man who receives a beating, the unnamed Samaritan who shows mercy,[3] the unnamed innkeeper (as an "essential" worker) who takes over the care of the stranger, and the lawyer (the only "real" person) who asks the question that leads to this parable.

Only the first one (the victim) has not yet received sufficient attention in this book, so a brief word is in order here. If Amy-Jill Levine is correct, the Jewish people in Jesus's audience would have seen themselves in the victim who was left half dead, not in the Samaritan. This victim represented all (Jewish) people. Many later interpreters attest to a similar approach (though less historical), finding in this character a broader representation of humanity.[4] Augustine discovered in this figure the allegorical representative of every spiritually lost soul, including his own. Howard Thurman described this person as one only half-conscious of the systemic racist divide into which someone "from the other side of the tracks" may bring support and healing. The Solentiname community in Nicaragua located in this

---

3. Even in recent biblical scholarship, the Samaritan continues to attract much attention; see Chalmers, "Rethinking Luke 10," 543–66.

4. Rare is the interpreter who would associate Jesus with the victim of the parable. Julian of Norwich (d. 1416) interpreted the parable in this way, finding God exemplified in the Samaritan's actions, a God who raised the victim from the dead (cited in Lischer, *Reading the Parables*, 154–55).

representative figure those on the political fringe of a capitalist system (supported by a mainstream church) that disenfranchises people even further. Harriet Jacobs associated the enslaved with this representative figure of the parable, even as she integrated the Samaritan character with the victim.

Readers may notice that I did not mention Jesus as one of the lives that mattered. Of course his life mattered too, but no reader (critical or otherwise) would actually misunderstand his prominence in this narrative. In fact, the life of Jesus is the most indispensable one within the Gospel of Luke. The entire sequence of events flows through his words and actions, his birth and death, and his teachings to his followers. No one has to make the case for what was obvious within Luke's story: Jesus's life mattered. The same cannot be said about the other figures; nevertheless, I would contend that their lives mattered too.

Treatment of the Other and "Salvation"

Jewish interpreters of this very Jewish story often suggest that the lawyer's question was contrived, because a first-century lawyer would never ask about "eternal life" in this manner.[5] The average Jewish person would have known that eternal life was determined by God's covenant with Israel and not by individual actions. Of course, a faithful Jew would have attempted to keep the commandments of Torah, but no individual law determined an individual's relationship to the God of Israel.

Christian interpreters often find in this story an emphasis on *doing* that seems a bit out of place with respect to the eternal life one hopes to secure. In many of these circles, salvation is defined as an activity that stems from confession and belief exclusively, epitomized best in the Pauline language of Romans 10:9–10: "If you confess with your lips that Jesus is Lord and believe in your heart that God raised him

5. Levine, *Short Stories by Jesus*, 85.

from the dead, you will be saved. For one believes with the heart and so is justified, and one confesses with the mouth and so is saved" (NRSV).

Distinct from this Pauline tradition (and the view of salvation the Romans passage implies) is that Jesus—in the Gospel of Luke—accepts the lawyer's question as sincere, turns his attention back to Torah, and fully accepts the man's response of the double-commandment of love. Love determines eternal life! Since love of God was not central to this inquiry, the lawyer apparently understood how one might practice love for the divine being. The story about Mary and Martha that follows may have provided a Lukan narrative example—"Mary has chosen the better part"—of what it means to love God (Luke 10:38–42).[6] Love for the neighbor, however, is the thornier concern. Jesus's parable—in Luke's account—seems to address the neighbor theme.

At the heart of this conversation lies a fundamental concern about the nature of salvation. As important as confession and belief are, salvation is also about *doing*. God's relationship with God's followers is not simply to bring them into God's presence in order to enjoy them. God has expectations for the people of God while they are on earth. "Do this and you will live," Jesus says (Luke 10:28). "*Do* this" is a clear reference to the commands of Torah. *Do* the actions required by Torah as a commitment to God and to neighbor. Be active in the doing. For Bishop Desmond Tutu, this Christian practice is the idea of *ubuntu*, the South African concept that assumes that one person's humanity is bound up intimately in the humanity of others.[7]

Yet not all doing is God's doing. "Do *this*," Jesus says. The "this," of course, points to the claims of Torah/Scripture. The "this" is love, a love that is inclusive of God and others. It is a love that pushes us to think very seriously about how we treat others. It is the second part of the "this" that the lawyer will question further. The lawyer

6. Edwards, *Luke's Story of Jesus*, 57.
7. Tutu, *No Future without Forgiveness*, 31–32.

and Jesus can each read Torah, but they must wrestle with Scripture together. The communal nature of this enterprise should not be lost on the contemporary reader.

Finally, doing connects with living. It is not simply that "you will live" *later*; "you will live" now, in the present moment, in the moment in which you find yourself. "Do this and you will live" out the calling to be the person God intended you to be. "You will live" to your fullest human potential when you recognize how connected to God you may become when you love your neighbor. The language of 1 John resonates here—even though it comes from a context in which there has been a church split: "Beloved, since God loved us so much, we also ought to love one another. No one has ever seen God; if we love one another, God lives in us, and his love is perfected in us" (1 John 4:11–12 NRSV).[8]

In many ways the lawyer's query is our own. It is a statement about the significance of one's life: Why am I here? If God exists, how do I live out my best life? How do I best stay connected to the creator of the universe? In response, Jesus intertwines Torah, love, God, community, and action. If we wish to connect to God, we need to treat one another in meaningful ways. "How do you read?"

As discussed in chapter 3, later in Luke's Gospel another character repeats the lawyer's initial question. The Lukan character is a leader who is wealthy (Luke 18:18–30). This is a sad tale that does not end well because the man is fond of his possessions. For our purposes here, I simply want to point out how the man's initial question about eternal life is connected to an expected action (care for the poor), which in turn leads even Jesus's closest followers to question, "Then who can be saved?" (18:26 NRSV). The disciples—much like many in later ecclesial communities—fail to appreciate that, as Luis Menéndez-Antuña observes, "theological salvation rests on political relations."[9]

---

8. For evidence of the church split, see 1 John 2:18–19. On love as central to the story, see Augustine and Thurman (chap. 2).

9. Menéndez-Antuña, "Black Lives Matter and Gospel Hermeneutics," 34.

In addition to the initial query about living, both stories express explicitly the role that followers of God should take in respect to others. One story is about an unknown neighbor; the second story is about the poor. Social actions toward others are fundamental to both stories and central to the mission of Luke's Jesus. In the Third Gospel, the Spirit-inspired Jesus (4:1, 14) reads from the words of Isaiah in his opening public sermon in his hometown and self-identifies with the one about whom he reads: "The Spirit of the Lord is upon me, because he has anointed me" (Luke 4:18 NRSV). Here the opening announcement points toward not only the identification of Jesus but also the activity of the anointed one: "He has anointed me to bring good news to the poor. He has sent me to proclaim release to the captives and recovery of sight to the blind, to let the oppressed go free" (4:18 NRSV). This language resonates as a potential motto for an ancient protest movement in the ancient Near Eastern world. The anointed one has come to reach out to the marginalized of his community: to people who are economically poor, to those who have been imprisoned under false pretenses or who are suffering lengthy sentences for misdemeanors, to people with physical ailments, to those who have suffered under oppressive regimes. This anointed one was God's agent on the scene to bring about change. The followers of Jesus—within the confines of the Lukan narrative—were expected to follow and march according to this anointed activity.

The Neighbor and the Body

Crucial to this story is the embodied faith it represents. Faith cannot be lived *outside the body*. Throughout the history of the Christian movement, there have been tensions over the active witness versus the contemplative witness. Many consider (correctly or not) the story of Mary, "who sat at the Lord's feet and listened to what he was saying," as Luke's support of the contemplative life ("Mary has chosen the better part," Luke 10:38–42 NRSV). Even if this were the case, one needs only to read the parable of the Samaritan, which precedes this story, to discover an account in support of the active life: "Go and do likewise" (10:37 NRSV).

Fundamental to this parable—and to the Gospel of Luke as a whole—is an emphasis on living out one's faith in relationship to others. The lawyer's question is the driving force for Jesus's parable: "Who is my neighbor?" The lawyer asks the pertinent question. He could have asked other questions: What does it mean to love God? What might be the relationship between love and the Christian disciplines? What does it mean to love one's self? How does self-care connect with Christian faithfulness? But the lawyer's question turns Jesus's (and the audience's) attention elsewhere. We are asked not to look upward toward God or to look inward toward ourselves but to look outward toward others. If the narrative of Luke 10 reflects a theological perspective, it is an embodied theology. *That is, one must act through the body for the sake of the physical well-being of another body.* This is the meaning of religious commitment. All kinds of religious persuasions may call for their members to participate in this kind of bodily activity. From my vantage point, this is what it means to be Christian. Confessions of love for the other are crucial; actions of love for the other are definitive. Practicing the confessions prepares one for the substantive acts of the faith.

The Gospel of Luke is a theological narrative about the body. Of course, the central character is Jesus, who is the embodiment of God on earth. To be certain, there is no Lukan language to match Matthew's explicit incarnational language, which Matthew draws from one of the prophets: "'Look, the virgin shall conceive and bear a son, and they shall name him Emmanuel,' which means, 'God is with us'" (Matt. 1:23 NRSV). For Luke, Jesus, as God's Son (Luke 1:35), is infused with God's Spirit to carry out the work of the Lord. Jesus is an embodied Spirit; more poignantly, he is a Spirit-embodied human being who "full of the Spirit" receives temptations (4:1) and "filled with the Spirit" enters his public ministry (4:14). Within this mission, Jesus makes lots of bodily contact with other bodies in need of healing; he is physically touching people all the time (5:13; 18:15; 22:51) and is expected to recognize what lies behind the touches of other people (7:39; 8:44–47). Furthermore, Jesus expects his followers to do the same; that is, they should continue his bodily acts of kindness toward others: "Whenever you enter a town, . . . cure the sick who are there" (10:8–9 NRSV).

The parable that has been the focus of this book is the gospel of embodied faith in miniature. The Samaritan saw another person, and the sight of the victim's plight—his condition, his brokenness, his physical bruises, the blood—moved the Samaritan's own body to make bodily contact. Those emotions pushed him into action, an action that required lots of bodily interaction: he bandaged his wounds, he put him on his own animal, and he took care of him. This bodily contact cost him time, money, and commitment.

During a season like a pandemic, Christians sense more clearly how *bodily* centric their faith is. When we are unable to touch one another with welcoming hugs or warm handshakes, when we are unable "to give the peace" to others in person, we can sense the loss of human contact. Many have elderly parents they are unable to visit. Many elderly care facilities are unable to allow human contact during this season.

Recently, I attended a virtual funeral service.[10] On the one hand, in light of travel restrictions, it was an opportunity at least to be part of the service. On the other hand, on this solemn occasion I wanted to be able to greet the loved ones in person, to give a comforting hug to the family members of the deceased. On a positive note, even if only virtually, I was able to hear stories of this blessed saint, stories about his encouragement to his siblings, his love for his children and grandchildren, his partnership with and support for his spouse in her own battles against patriarchal structures, and, over and over again, his fight against racist structures within the church. I was encouraged

10. For Dr. John Stanley, who was my colleague in the Department of Biblical and Religious Studies at Messiah University.

by hearing these stories, many of which I did not know. My former colleague was the first white professor I had known who used *True to Our Native Land* as a textbook in his courses to help his white students think more deeply about their faith and the wide variety of expression within the Christian movement.[11] But I was saddened to be unable to be physically present. In Christian circles, the body matters. In life and in death, the body matters. We have an embodied faith into which we need to live constantly. Jesus's parable of the Samaritan is a creative reminder of how much the body matters.

Parable as a Creative Example of Faith through Story

Fundamental to the Luke 10 story is the fact that it is a *parable*. Historians of Jesus agree that Jesus was a parable teacher. He used them often, despite what readers find in the Fourth Gospel (which records no parables).[12] As mentioned in chapter 1, Luke and Matthew expand what is found in the Gospel of Mark. Most of Luke's unique parables fall within what is called his "travel narrative" (9:51–19:27).[13] More significant for our purposes in this final chapter is the nature of the parable discourse itself.

The parable is a creative tool Jesus utilized to relay his thoughts about God's activity in the world, human interactions, and the values he put forward for those who desired to follow his teaching. Nonetheless, even among these engaging short stories, the one about the Samaritan's actions stands out. It is rare for Jesus to place the "other" as the hero of one his stories.

As a point of comparison, it was not uncommon for Jesus to present two primary characters in his parables to compare one character's

11. Blount et al., *True to Our Native Land*.

12. Although the word "parable" (*parabolē*) does not occur in the Fourth Gospel, John 10:1–6 may be one. Note the use of "proverb" or "figure of speech" (*paroimia*) at 10:6.

13. Jesus's journey toward Jerusalem bookends the narrative unit: "When the days drew near for him to be taken up, he set his face to go to Jerusalem" (Luke 9:51). "After he had said this, he went on ahead, going up to Jerusalem" (19:28).

actions to the other's. He compared a Jewish man's two sons to each other, beginning with the one who requested a share of his inheritance in advance (Luke 15:11–32). He compared an unnamed wealthy man to Lazarus, a poor man who desired to eat crumbs from the wealthy man's table (16:19–31). He told the story of an unjust judge and a persistent widow who continually requested justice (18:1–8). There is also the story about two people who go into the temple to pray, a Pharisee and a tax collector (18:9–14). So in the Jewish context of Jesus's day, all these figures were common characters who were representative of the kind of people Jewish hearers would know all too well.

To appreciate the twist Jesus intended in each account, today's readers should attempt to understand how the parable might have struck its audience oddly. Many of the stories challenge cultural expectations by imagining alternative scenarios. It is odd that any child would initiate a request for an inheritance before the death of the parents.[14] Many Jewish people with wealth would generally care for the Lazaruses near their homes. Judges would not keep their local positions for long if they cared little about justice (in the first century!). A tax collector who offered a humble prayer—while possible and even likely—would surprise most in light of tax collectors' unfavorable reputations among the general populace. In the same manner, we must appreciate what is odd about the parable in Luke 10.

The Samaritan story is not a miniature fictional parable about an individual protagonist, as if the Samaritan trader could actually serve as the hero for the common Jews of Judea.[15] This is not even a story about the Torah as hero (i.e., "the one who does Torah . . ."), although Jesus's Samaritan did prove himself to be the one who carried out the commands of Torah more than the priest and the Levite. Rather, it is a story about human dignity. One person treats another person in

14. Also Nolland, *Luke 9:21–18:34*, 782.
15. See, however, the recent challenge to the traditional view of the Samaritan as a non-Jewish other and enemy of the Jewish people in Chalmers, "Rethinking Luke 10," 543–66.

need the way one would wish to be treated in that scenario. Moreover, the one with whom the *Jewish* audience would relate—the victim in this case[16]—must be willing to accept the kind acts of a *Samaritan*. Surprisingly, in the larger story in chapter 10, Luke does not grant Jesus the final word. The author allows the lawyer to speak one final time in a response to Jesus's query. Indeed, if the lawyer has read the law all his life, he already knows the answer he is about to repeat.

Consequently, the Samaritan parable fits nicely into the general pattern of other parables. It, too, likely surprised its audiences, turning upside down what was the common experience of most first-century Jewish people. In one way, however, it stands out. Although many of Jesus's characters who have less access (or respect) in society—the widow, the poor, the tax collector—receive elevation of honor within Luke's account, all of them are Jewish people. Within this group of parables, the Samaritan is unique as a character with whom Jesus's Jewish audience would find it difficult to identify. As some interpreters have suggested, this may explain why the lawyer's final response did not name the Samaritan as such but simply referred to him as "the one who showed mercy." Of all the characters within the Lukan parables, including even the tax collector, the Samaritan is the least sympathetic figure for a Jewish audience. As the passage about the healed lepers (which is a story unique to Luke) highlights, a Samaritan was considered—in the words of Jesus—a "foreigner" (*allogenēs*; 17:18) within the Lukan narrative.

The parable itself is a creative example of how to express and think about faith in story form. The contemporary church should follow this lead and think about how the stories of its members (warts and all) make up the various theological expressions of its body. The church should come to appreciate the messiness of stories and how oftentimes many of the pieces of a story do not neatly fit into any preconceived systems of thought. It is a story, after all, even while a story also expresses the nature of the human experience. Moreover, in the midst of

16. Nolland, *Luke 9:21–18:34*, 592; Levine, *Short Stories by Jesus*, 94–95.

our lives, in the midst of our stories, strange things often occur, some real and some imagined. What are the stories that we attempt to tell? Whom do they include? Do they always fit the expected patterns of our theologies? Should they? Or, once in a while, are we creative enough or, more importantly, bold enough to tell a story in which the "hero" is not who anyone would expect? Do we have bold enough imaginations to wonder if God just might be bigger and more inclusive than what we have allowed in our company so far? Might we imagine a church, a community, a family, a world in which those who have been historically, culturally, and theologically excluded might have a place in our parables and in our public spaces? Our religious spaces will not change if we cannot alter our imaginations.[17] A common saying these days is "Be the change you want to see." Perhaps before we are able to do that, we have to *imagine* the change we want to see. We have to visualize and put into creative efforts—songs, art, plays, children's books—heroes who do not look like us, believe like us, or love like us. People who are not us are loved by the God of love! Imagine that! A parable—Jesus's parable about a Samaritan—may just be the starting point we need to imagine a future that looks different from the present. Who do you imagine to be the hero of *your* story?

▨ The Church and Good Trouble: BLM and the Church's Response

There are at least two ways to look at the parable of Luke 10. First, it is a story about an individual's response to another individual in need. In fact, many of the so-called Good Samaritan Laws of contemporary US society relate to the parable in this manner, albeit with attention focused less on the victim than on the Samaritan who then can assist others in crisis without fear of litigation if their actions accidentally lead to more injury.[18]

---

17. Cf. Duckworth, *Wide Welcome*; Duncan, *Dear Church*; Hart, *Who Will Be a Witness?*

18. Here is an example from New Jersey's Good Samaritan Law: "Those individuals who, acting in good faith, voluntarily attempted to provide medical assistance

Second, this story could also be understood as representative of a community's response to other communities. The two interpretations are not incompatible with each other. But the latter viewpoint takes much more seriously the representative nature of the characters within a parable. Did Jesus's unnamed but ethnically labeled Samaritan matter for the thrust of the story? As an imaginative exercise, could Jesus be thinking about larger interactions between people groups? As mentioned several times throughout this book, the Jewish audience listening to these parables would have expected Jesus to use a common Jewish person who was (for the purposes of the parable) formally unrestrained by the religious institution (represented by the priest and Levite). If the audience's expectations had been met in this way, they would have grasped the importance of their individual actions and also a potential critique of the religious leadership associated with the Jerusalem temple. The setting, after all, is on a road "going down from Jerusalem" (Luke 10:30). Jesus, however, offers a twist on these expectations by highlighting the geographical and ethnic identity of the hero of the story. This, of course, would have caused his audience pause—as it should for us!

Was the parable an attempt to disturb the peace of his community for the good of others? Was Jesus's creative storytelling—to imagine a Samaritan (an enemy foreigner) instead of one of his own—an intentional act to disrupt the status quo?[19] It would not be surprising if it were, since his parables often functioned in this way.

Rev. Dr. Martin Luther King Jr. offered several sermons and speeches for which this parable provided the impetus. In one speech, King's entire vision of societal transformation may best be encapsulated in his reflection on Jesus's parable of the good Samaritan.

---

to those in need will be immune from legal liability and prosecution regarding any act or omission with respect to the accident victim." See Ferrara Law Firm, "What You Need to Know."

19. On the link between this parable and Jesus's teaching to love one's enemies, Joel Green reflects, "The point is not that we will not generate boundaries, but that we cannot expect that God will honor them" (*Theology of the Gospel of Luke*, 139).

King understood how important it is for individuals to show acts of kindness to neighbors, but he also determined that the story could encourage its audience beyond individual change. His own twist on the story is worth repeating here (see chap. 2): "One day the whole Jericho Road must be transformed so that men and women will not be beaten and robbed as they make their journey through life. True compassion is more than flinging a coin to a beggar; it understands that an edifice which produces beggars needs restructuring."[20] Jesus's original parable addressed the query "Who is my neighbor?" in striking ways. King reinterpreted this parable as the initial act of a journey that eventually requires a willingness to challenge and renovate the structural, unjust systems that would allow for acts of robbery in the first place. King summoned this parable to assist in his critique of America's insistence on the value of the Vietnam War. Many of his African American colleagues thought King's participation in the anti-war effort distracted from the more important task of addressing societal racism. King, however, saw the intersectional nature of America's three big evils: militarism, racism, and economic exploitation. The biblical story fueled his Christian imagination, and his imagination invented a new world in the present. Since a just world did not exist, the first step—in King's mind—was to visualize it. Those who love a literal interpretation of biblical stories and subsequently attempt to apply such literalism will be disappointed with King's approach here and elsewhere.[21] Jesus's imagination fueled King's own. King's good Samaritan story included a step beyond the original story itself, and he developed his own "parable," one in which the biblical account needed to be reconstructed to begin the development of a new, just world in the present: "the whole Jericho Road must be transformed." In his reading of the parable, King advocated for "good trouble."[22]

20. King, *Where Do We Go from Here*, 198.
21. See Powery and Powery, "King, the Bible, and the 'World House.'"
22. "Good trouble" was John Lewis's phrase for fighting for freedom and equality for all people.

There are good examples of good trouble, even among the religious.[23] One of King's lieutenants, John Lewis, passed away in the summer of 2020. As a lifelong advocate for change in civil rights actions and legislation, Lewis was without equal. Prior to his death, he wrote an editorial opinion piece, with an agreement to publish it on the day of this death, titled "Together, You Can Redeem the Soul of Our Nation." His audience was the present-day marchers for justice. As he puts it, "Emmett Till was my George Floyd. He was my Rayshard Brooks, Sandra Bland and Breonna Taylor." Lewis advocates that *church* people and all people of goodwill must be about "good trouble, necessary trouble." Lewis acknowledges the ongoing nature of the political enterprise, which involves persistent action: "Democracy is not a state; it is an act." He even uses theological language to express his concerns. The nation has a "soul" that must be "redeemed," and he directs his political, rhetorical, theological appeals to the ecclesial wings of this country's citizens.[24] The life and work of Lewis should force those of us with ecclesial commitments to ask, Is the church engaged in good trouble?

One white Catholic priest (Sam Sawyer, SJ) advocates for good trouble in light of the link he sees between the BLM movement and the good Samaritan story. His short 2016 magazine essay (four years *before* the death of George Floyd and Breonna Taylor), "Who Became a Neighbor? Reading Black Lives Matter through the Good Samaritan," reads like a public confession. The connection between this parable and the BLM movement stems from Sawyer's theological understanding of speaking on behalf of those on the margins of

23. Religious people who spend their time and energy attacking the nonreligious nature of the BLM movement expose their own privilege in a society in which the rights and liberties of the disenfranchised—whether that is due to race, class, or sexual preference—are protected less by the structures that have been put in place.

24. In his published remembrance, "A Personal Tribute to My Friend John Lewis," Bishop Nathan Baxter reminds us that Lewis was an ordained, seminary-trained minister.

society, or what he refers to theologically as "the preferential option for the poor."[25] As he puts it, this is a theological attempt "to cooperate in God's work of making its [the gospel's] promises real for them." Here is one of Sawyer's brutally honest confessions: "If Jesus in the Gospel calls me to become a neighbor, the first step is to get out on the road. I don't, at this moment, have a concrete plan for doing that, and all sorts of excuses present themselves to avoid making such plans. Some of the excuses are better than others. None of them are good enough."[26] Sawyer recognizes that all people of goodwill have to take initial steps in order to participate in good trouble.

Along the way (remember, this was published in 2016!), Sawyer discovered that there are several police departments attempting to revise their policies surrounding the use of force. Many of us tend to ignore that this conversation has been going on for a long time, even while acknowledging that these revisions alone will not dismantle the racism buried deep within the structures of so many US institutions. One final confession from Sawyer is in order here: "Today, in our society, this means paying attention to the threats to black lives *as they are experienced by black people.* We need to learn that the insufficiency of our good intentions and personal non-racism is not a rejection of their goodness, but a call to solidarity in a struggle led by others."[27] The church must ask itself if it is engaged in good trouble.

My original plan was to choose the most theologically minded, most ecclesially leaning member of the three BLM leaders and write this short section. Then I stumbled onto *Time*'s list of the one hundred most influential people of 2020. It is not striking to find Alicia

25. Sawyer, "Who Became a Neighbor?" According to liberation theology, this theological idea resonates with "Mary's song" in Luke's narrative: "He has brought down the powerful from their thrones, and lifted up the lowly; he has filled the hungry with good things, and sent the rich away empty" (Luke 1:52–53).

26. Sawyer, "Who Became a Neighbor?"

27. Sawyer, "Who Became a Neighbor?" (his italics).

Garza, Patrisse Cullors, and Opal Tometi selected; what is striking is how rare their approach to leadership is. *Time*'s selection epitomizes the post-Enlightenment, Western emphasis on the individual leader among its "influential people." That is the dominant leadership model in the United States. For those of us who are American Christians, this cultural slant also affects the way we read the Bible. The collective leadership model (as exemplified by the work of Garza, Cullors, and Tometi), on the other hand, stands at the heart of the BLM movement and should stand as an extraordinary example of the meaning of true change in a society in which individuals are often elevated to positions of authority, power, and influence that many of them did not earn on their own. In most meaningful, long-lasting efforts, it "takes a village."

The BLM movement has been about good trouble in its insistence on necessary change for the most vulnerable in today's society. A brief acknowledgment in *Time* was written by Sybrina Fulton, the mother of Trayvon Martin, whose murder was the incident that provoked these three leaders to create the platforms for a national conversation (including the bodily engaged platform of the public protest) around three simple yet profound words: "black lives matter." Over the last several years, the BLM movement—with its multiracial and now global efforts—has called into question the nation's response to the relationship among police enforcement, race, and this country's history.[28] As one recent public service announcement declared, "All lives can't matter until black lives matter." Such a sentiment should be the rallying cry of every local ecclesial and religious community in which people confess to care for others.[29]

28. Sybrina Fulton's home is only a few miles away from my childhood home in Miami, where my parents still reside. I can recall vividly the first conversation I had with my mother after Trayvon Martin's death. My mother spoke to me as if Fulton was a next-door neighbor and Martin used to play in our driveway. I was struck by my mother's rightly just response to this tragedy. Indeed, Martin was our neighbor but had no "Samaritan" to aid him on that fateful day.

29. For a reading of Luke's Gospel (especially chaps. 7–8) that attempts to take black subjectivity and the BLM movement seriously as a theoretical framework, see Menéndez-Antuña, "Black Lives Matter and Gospel Hermeneutics."

For some Christians, the BLM movement is an expression of (Christian?) faith in action.[30] Lewis's visit to Black Lives Matter Plaza was his final public appearance.[31] In other ecclesial quarters, it has become customary to wonder about potential alliances between the BLM movement and the church. Many of these concerns have come from predominantly white church institutions, but they have not been entirely absent from some of the more conservative-leaning black congregations as well.[32] As Hebah Farrag stresses, "Some see BLM as secularizing the new civil rights movement."[33] Farrag's defense of the organizational structure of the BLM movement may explain some of these reactions: "The BLM network has embraced female and queer leadership along with membership often shunned and/or marginalized by traditional faith groups, thus disrupting a legacy of civil rights leadership that is largely hetero-normative and almost exclusively male."[34]

In some ecclesial quarters, as Jennifer Leath, a scholar of religion and a pastor, observes when reviewing the historical record, the (black?) church frequently expresses "ambivalence" when responding to racial justice issues and should use this opportunity to "listen" and "learn" from the BLM movement. Their ambivalence is not about naming the racial injustice; their hesitancy is about the proper methods for a response.[35] Leath calls on those less engaged politically to utilize their best practices even now: "The best that pastoral care, religious ethics, and theology have to offer right now is a persistent, activating, practicable, and survival-oriented critique of religiosities and societies that perpetuate domination power models, othering, origin veiling, and unacknowledged subjectivity. Religious practitioners

---

30. Hart, *Who Will Be a Witness?*, 296.
31. Baxter, "Personal Tribute to My Friend John Lewis."
32. E.g., Oppenheimer, "Some Evangelicals Struggle."
33. Farrag, "Fight for Black Lives."
34. Farrag, "Fight for Black Lives."
35. Leath, "Perpetual Cycle of However."

can sit at the feet of the leaderful streets: Listen, learn, and act to end the injustice of sinful sufferings that result from social organizations and relationships built with primordial premises of person(s)-over-person(s)."[36] Along with Sawyer, Leath advocates for the church to take on the role of the Lukan character Mary, who sat at Jesus's feet, to "listen" to the "streets" and then to develop the kind of courageous consciousness that allows them to participate in acts of good trouble.

Reenvisioning Theological Education

In addition to active participation in the protests across the nation, many church leaders and members are attempting to listen to the streets, as Leath suggests. The commission on accrediting for the Association for Theological Schools—the leading organization for theological schools—sponsored one such seminar to listen to four prominent African American theologians (Kelly Brown Douglas, Willie Jennings, Stephen Ray, and Emilie Townes) on the impact racial justice should have on theological training and its curriculum.[37] Less than one month after George Floyd's murder, the tone of the event was as striking as the content they shared. Reflecting critically on the overall composition and particular elements of the curriculum and practices of institutions while individual black bodies are violated in the streets can be an overwhelming and emotionally challenging task. The tone was clear: something *must* change. Similar to King's reflection on the parable: "the whole Jericho Road must be transformed." These theologians agreed: traditional white theology is the "Jericho Road" of contemporary theological education.

As these theologians collectively stressed, truth telling is fundamental to the theological enterprise, and traditional white theology

---

36. Leath, "Perpetual Cycle of However." In a more sermonic tone she continues, "How tragic it is to conclude that the fight for racial justice is a *soul* fight—and that *religion* is most unprepared to equip those unable to breathe through the suffocating force of knee on neck!" (her italics).

37. "Black Lives Matter: Where Do We Go from Here?"

has failed to promote the truth in its work and has supported white supremacy (Douglas). This inherited theology is incapable, as Townes poignantly points out, of answering the question of how violence on black bodies continues into the twenty-first century. If we follow Townes's direction, what does it mean if traditional theology is unable to answer today's most crucial questions about some of the most vulnerable among us?

Part of the truth-telling work is to admit, in Ray's words, that one's white ancestors were "moral monsters."[38] Not beginning with that (theological!) confession leads descendants to offer attempts at a defense (even theologically) of their ancestors' practices; these are efforts to discover why they did what they did, while placing the blame elsewhere. This point exposes the ongoing debates around Confederate monuments: What do these symbols continue to represent for the US citizenry? The legacies of the early hierarchical, patriarchal, and racial structures in the US have bequeathed to us unjust legacies in which we continue to live and do theological training. Theological training centers must jettison this particular colonial theological agenda. This bold move requires a collective theological will. As Willie Jennings might put it, we have "failed to enter into the revolutionary life of Jesus."[39] Shortly after the murders of Breonna Taylor (March 13, 2020) and George Floyd (May 25, 2020) in state-sanctioned violence, the visceral cries of these theologians can still be heard in their critique of the theological enterprise in which they find themselves. Theological training has a direct impact on the types of theological pastors these institutions send into our churches and, thereby, on how those leaders will engage the discipleship practices of our local ecclesial assemblies.

---

38. "Black Lives Matter: Where Do We Go from Here?" Moreover, on this panel Ray emphasizes how our theologies shape *political* action; we must take physical bodies seriously.

39. Gerd Theissen, a biblical scholar far removed from this conversation, observes in a similar fashion, "I often ask myself why Jesus counts so little among great theologians. . . . But could it not be that there has always been a suspicion that once one admits the historical Jesus one admits a proclamation aimed at changes not only in the church but also throughout society?" *Shadow of the Galilean*, 95.

Undeniably, this conversation has been going on for some time in theological circles. In 2016 the *Christian Century* published a "report" in which a number of theologians, theological ethicists, and scholars of religion offered reflections on violence against black bodies within the United States.[40] Since that time the *Christian Century* has continued to publish short reflections on the BLM movement. Since these initial conversations, recent religious and theological reflections have become more attentive to the BLM movement. Cleve Tinsley IV, a scholar of American religion, race, and culture, is one example. Similar to Townes, Tinsley concludes, "Religious communities can no longer gloss over the reality that white supremacist hetero-patriarchy and racial capitalism, along with all of the menacing effects entrained with them, is founded upon a virulent, death-dealing anti-Blackness."[41]

This critique is not exclusive to black scholars of religion. As theological ethicist Elizabeth Bounds, a member of white Protestant Christianity and a theological educator, describes the kind of education that has been complicit in the present state of affairs, "We white Protestants face the challenge that so many of our traditions and symbols have been shaped by white supremacy. We are reluctant to interrogate our particular Christian heritage, refusing to see its complicity in black suffering. Our theological understandings of reconciliation or the 'colorblind' communion of God's children can paper over realities of power and histories of white domination. But some white Christian leaders are trying to break open the truth by naming the specifics of racial history and rereading their Christian legacy."[42] Sadly, not all white Christian leaders encourage their religious communities to wrestle honestly with this racial history. According to a Public Religion Research Institute survey, fewer white evangelical Christians

40. "Black Lives Matter." Contributors included Brian Bantum, Anthea Butler, Brittney Cooper, Gary Dorrien, Jennifer Harvey, Eboni Marshall Turman, and Reggie Williams.
41. Tinsley, "Amid Phantoms of Death."
42. Bounds, "Joining the Sinners or Resisting the Sin?"

believe that the historical, institutional structures themselves are racist than their nonreligious white counterparts.[43] This tension creates a challenge for collective efforts to review, revise, and in some cases dismantle theological systems that have a long history of obstructing a more just and equitable training for pastors and other future religious leaders. As a sidenote, I would add that racial assumptions also impact the way we engage Scripture; there is a direct correlation between our communal reading practices of the Bible and how we view the world in which we live.

Because of that general failure to revise theological education, the new movement of "young activists," as Cleve Tinsley IV acknowledges, poses a challenge to church communities.[44] The history of the US church reveals that the church has not always stood on the side of the powerless socially and politically, despite the church's theological commitments. Even in this moment, faith communities could learn from the way these young activists encourage the redistribution of organizing power to the populations most directly affected by the inequities of our day.[45]

On the Theological Practices of the Church

What is the immediate impact of theological education on the churches that we attend? Of course, in the United States there are many independent churches that require little to no formal theological education for their ministers. This does not mean there is no theological education; the education is, however, less formal, less organized, and more through an individual's own choices of literature and teachers. That is, the developing theology may become less

43. Quoted in Jones, "Racism among White Christians."
44. Tinsley, "Amid Phantoms of Death."
45. Tinsley continues with this word of caution in "Amid Phantoms of Death": "It will be impossible for many religious practitioners to do this effectively if they are not open to moving past some of the inherent dogmatism and moral superiority in their traditions that have come to define and bind them in community."

responsible to the communal faith we call Christian. Those groups, too, are part of what makes up American Christianity. Perhaps it is more accurate to describe our present context as one occupied by American Christianities. Nevertheless, it is the responsibility of faith communities to participate in the good of society, even perhaps, as Kelly Brown Douglas suggests, to lead toward a more just future.[46]

Yet the first act should not be a rush toward reconciliation (per Townes)[47] but rather to name the injustice, confess our histories, and recognize the sources that contribute to the violence. We must call out the evil before we can acknowledge the good. This public announcement is also part of what it means to participate in good trouble. We must come to appreciate the diversity among us, to claim this difference as a theological gift. Difference is good, theologically speaking. To put it another way, God created difference![48] Or as Cheryl Sanders puts it, "Do black lives matter to God?"[49] In the spirit of this book, Jesus's imaginative use of the Samaritan confirms the creative power of difference to challenge the status quo of our lives together.

46. "Black Lives Matter: Where Do We Go from Here?"

47. "Black Lives Matter: Where Do We Go from Here?"

48. I am thinking in broader theological terms here, rather than with the view that a "biblical God" is the only available construct for theological reflection. To believe the latter uncritically fails to appreciate the complex nature of our biblical narratives and the complex histories to which they point. Along these lines, see Josiah Ulysses Young III's reflections in his contribution to the 2020 Berkley Forum, "'Many Thousands Gone'": "Deeper scrutiny of the texts unveils, however, that the Hebrew Bible's YHWH favors men over women and Shem's sons over Ham's. In precisely what way, then, are 'all men created equal,' and when did we lose this equality, why, and according to whom? Perhaps those questions might move us to shelve the ethnocentric myths we have devised to empower ourselves against others. Americans should never forget that upholders of slavery legitimized their avarice biblically and thus saw themselves as YHWH's New World elect."

49. C. Sanders, "Do Black Lives Matter to God?"

Conclusion

Imagining a "Samaritan" for the Life of the Church

Following Wil Gafney's and Richard Newton's insights in their contributions to a special forum on the potential implications of the BLM movement for the field of biblical studies,[1] it is intriguing to reflect on Jesus's use of the Samaritan. In our discourse, do we ever include conversations, teaching, or words of wisdom from people unlike us? Do we include Muslims, Jews, transgender people, queer people, or immigrants? Must our heroes always look like us, love like us, and share our values? Is it possible to conceive of the dignity of another who is most unlike us?

In addition to the parable, Jesus's initial response to the lawyer remains key: "How do you read?" In trying to understand the *Lukan* view—that is, to read the biblical passage within its original context—interpreters should think through a number of factors in Luke's narrative: his treatment of "lawyers"; his view of ethnic groups (i.e., Samaritans); the parables of Jesus; interactions between Jesus and

---

1. Gafney, "Reflection on the Black Lives Matter Movement"; Newton, "African American Bible." Other contributors to this special forum included Bernadette Brooten, Nyasha Junior, Kenneth Ngwa, and Tat-siong Benny Liew.

Jewish leaders; Luke's larger ethnic ideology in Luke-Acts; and Luke's themes compared with other Synoptic Gospels.

Within this book (see chap. 3), I have attempted to tackle several of these themes in order to place Luke 10 within a larger Lukan context. But there is more to how we read Scripture in the life of the church than our attempts to engage the biblical text as if we were reading it for the first time. There are traditions that shape our ecclesiological communities, and we may or may not be aware of them. My effort in chapter 2 was an attempt to capture a snapshot of some of these traditions and reading strategies that have come down to us, some more familiar to us than others, depending on the church tradition to which we belong. Those interpretive traditions often lie behind many of the assumptions we make about particular biblical themes or characters. Then, finally, within the final chapter I have attempted to connect particular elements of the "original" story—in light of the tradition(s) of the church and an engagement with Luke's Gospel context—with specific theological concepts that seem most crucial to our contemporary moment. Perhaps in this chapter readers have sensed my theological bias most clearly. In any case, the goal of this volume has been to ask the broader question about faithful practice as it connects to the way we think about God (theology). In that spirit, does our reading call forth an embodied faith? Does our interpretation move us to act on behalf of others?

It should not go unnoticed that this entire book project is a *theological* investigation into a parable, a story Jesus made up, a story he constructed from his imagination, a story that has led to the naming of many real-life organizations (e.g., the Good Samaritan Museum, Samaritan's Purse, Samaritan Center) in the contemporary world. Nonetheless, it is a simple story about a common event: robbers beat and rob a man; some presumably respectable folks walk past him; one disreputable person surprisingly stops to assist, and he commits time and money to help. The end!

In the midst of his own critical moment, Jesus says, "Samaritan lives matter." Well, perhaps the lawyer may have been thinking "all lives matter," with the assumption that "all" refers primarily to Jewish lives.[2] But Jesus did not merely select any person to play the lead role of his now famous parable. He chose a Samaritan; SLM was his cry!

Our religious spaces will not change if we cannot alter our imaginations. Perhaps before we are able to rethink our communities, we have to *imagine* the change we want to see. We have to visualize and put into practice the possibility that people who do not share our class, our race, our ethnic background, our religion, our sexual preference, or our ideology might contribute something meaningful to the spaces we inhabit. God loves people that we have not yet developed the capacity to love. A rereading of Jesus's parable about a Samaritan may provide an opportunity to imagine a future that looks different from the present. How do you read?

I've Never Lost Hope

I can't believe he returned! I told Abdul, my brother, that the man would not come back to repay us for what we would spend to assist the injured man back to health. Abdul wanted to send the partially healed man off after a day or two and said to me, "He'll be fine. His eyesight has returned, and he's able to walk on his own again."

From the way he said it, without looking at me, I was certain he wanted the man gone for other reasons. Perhaps because he is gay, or perhaps because he is Jewish. I knew we could not send him off in his condition. He was not ready to travel back to his town on his own. So I told Abdul, "OK, I do not disagree with you completely, but since I'm still unsure, I will walk with him for the first ten miles. Then, he can travel the rest of the way on his own."

That was enough for my overly protective brother to exclaim, "OK, OK! We'll keep him for a couple more days."

2. Perhaps Jesus the Jew would be forgiven for this claim, but would Luke the gentile?

I thought for sure we would not recover any financial assistance from the white nationalist who promised, "I'll pay you back for what you've spent when I return." When I first overheard him say this to Abdul, and overheard the tone with which he said it, I just rolled my eyes. We have heard so many of these kinds of promises before from these types of people.

Then, a few days later he showed up. I couldn't believe he came back! Not only had he returned, but he repaid us twice as much as we spent despite our efforts to refuse the additional amount. To be honest, I didn't want *his* money. He said he wanted to do this because his business travels took twice as long as he thought they would originally. He apologized for putting us in this predicament. Then his final comment really stunned me. He said, "I will take the man back to his home."

I know that he lives in the opposite direction of the man's family, since our hotel is halfway between their hometowns. When I heard this news, I thought to myself, "God works in mysterious ways."

My next (selfish?) thought was, "Perhaps God will even change Abdul's mind again, and he'll return to the faith of our parents." In my heart, I've never lost hope.

Bibliography

"An Amish America Q-and-A with Professor David Weaver-Zercher." *Amish America*, September 18, 2008. http://amishamerica.com/an-amish-america -q-and-a-with-professor-david-weaver-zercher/.

Anderson, Robert. "Samaritans." In *The New Interpreter's Dictionary of the Bible*, edited by Katharine Doob Sakenfeld, 5:75–82. Nashville: Abingdon, 2009.

Aymer, Margaret. "Acts of the Apostles." In *Women's Bible Commentary*, 20th anniv. ed., edited by Carol A. Newsom, Sharon H. Ringe, and Jacqueline E. Lapsley, 536–46. Louisville: Westminster John Knox, 2012.

Baker, Cynthia. "From Every Nation under Heaven: Jewish Ethnicities in the Greco-Roman World." In *Prejudice and Christian Beginnings: Investigating Race, Gender and Ethnicity in Early Christian Studies*, edited by Laura Nasrallah and Elisabeth Schüssler Fiorenza, 79–99. Minneapolis: Fortress, 2009.

Barreto, Eric. "Except This Foreigner?" *Sojourners*, October 3, 2016. https:// sojo.net/articles/except-foreigner.

———. "Whence Migration? Babel, Pentecost, and Biblical Imagination." In *Latinxs, the Bible, and Migration*, edited by Efraín Agosto and Jacqueline M. Hidalgo, 133–47. Cham, Switzerland: Palgrave Macmillan, 2018.

Barron, Robert. "Forgiving Dylann Roof." *First Things*, March 2017. https:// www.firstthings.com/article/2017/03/forgiving-dylann-roof.

Baxter, Nathan. "A Personal Tribute to My Friend John Lewis." *Penn-Live: Patriot News*, July 24, 2020. https://www.pennlive.com/opinion/2020/07 /a-personal-tribute-to-a-friend-bishop-nathan-baxter.html.

Bennett, Lerone, Jr. "Howard Thurman: 20th Century Holy Man." *Ebony*, February 1978.

————. *What Manner of Man: A Biography of Martin Luther King, Jr.* Chicago: Johnson, 1964.

Betz, H. D. "The Cleansing of the Ten Lepers." *Journal of Biblical Literature* 90, no. 3 (1971): 314–28.

"Black Lives Matter." *The Christian Century*, March 8, 2016. https://www.christiancentury.org/article/2016-02/seven-writers-assess-movement.

"Black Lives Matter: Where Do We Go from Here?" ATSCOA, June 17, 2020. YouTube video, 1:29:54. https://www.youtube.com/watch?v=KZ IF5Oijw9M&fbclid=IwAR2rqABANiQLO_eV513QTUJ4A94ZRbFk3 dipV51rQ3MyYaNtoznvu-Sa01M.

Blight, David W. *Frederick Douglass: Prophet of Freedom*. New York: Simon & Schuster, 2018.

Bloom, Sandra L. "Trauma Theory Abbreviated." In *Final Action Plan: A Coordinated, Community-Based Response to Family Violence*, by Attorney General Mike Fisher's Family Violence Task Force. Harrisburg: Pennsylvania Office of Attorney General, 1999. https://www.aipro.info/wp/wp-content/uploads/2017/08/Trauma_theory_abbreviated.pdf.

Blount, Brian K. "The Souls of Biblical Folks and the Potential for Meaning." *Journal of Biblical Literature* 138, no. 1 (2019): 6–21.

————. *Then the Whisper Put on Flesh: New Testament Ethics in an African American Context*. Nashville: Abingdon, 2001.

Blount, Brian K., Cain Hope Felder, Clarice J. Martin, and Emerson B. Powery, eds. *True to Our Native Land: An African American New Testament Commentary*. Minneapolis: Fortress, 2007.

Bounds, Elizabeth. "Joining the Sinners or Resisting the Sin? American Christian Churches and Race." Berkley Forum, Berkley Center for Religion, Peace & World Affairs, Georgetown University, June 16, 2020. https://berkleycenter.georgetown.edu/responses/joining-the-sinners-or-resisting-the-sin-american-christian-churches-and-race.

Brawley, Robert L. *Luke-Acts and the Jews: Conflict, Apology, and Conciliation*. Atlanta: Scholars Press, 1987.

Braxton, Joanne M. *Black Women Writing Autobiography: A Tradition within a Tradition*. Philadelphia: Temple University Press, 1989.

Brown, Peter. *Augustine of Hippo: A Biography*. Berkeley: University of California Press, 1967.

———. *Religion and Society in the Age of Saint Augustine*. London: Faber & Faber, 1972.

Burrus, Virginia, and Catherine Keller. "Confessing Monica." In Stark, *Feminist Interpretations of Augustine*, 119–46.

Cardenal, Ernesto. *Abide in Love*. Maryknoll, NY: Orbis Books, 1995.

———. *The Gospel in Solentiname*. Translated by Donald D. Walsh. 4 vols. Maryknoll, NY: Orbis Books, 1979.

Carey, Greg. *Sinners: Jesus and His Earliest Followers*. Waco: Baylor University Press, 2009.

Carson, Sharon. "Dismantling the House of the Lord: Theology as Political Philosophy in *Incidents in the Life of a Slave Girl*." *Journal of Religious Thought* 51, no. 1 (1994): 53–66.

Carter, J. Kameron. *Race: A Theological Account*. Oxford: Oxford University Press, 2008.

Chadwick, Henry. *Augustine of Hippo: A Life*. Oxford: Oxford University Press, 2009.

Chalmers, Matthew. "Rethinking Luke 10: The Parable of the Good Samaritan Israelite." *Journal of Biblical Literature* 139, no. 3 (2020): 543–66.

Clark, Patrick. "Reversing the Ethical Perspective: What the Allegorical Interpretation of the Good Samaritan Parable Can Still Teach Us." *Theology Today* 71, no. 3 (October 2014): 300–309.

Cohen, Shaye J. D. *From the Maccabees to the Mishnah*. Louisville: Westminster John Knox, 2006.

Collins, Adela Yarbro. *Mark: A Commentary*. Minneapolis: Fortress, 2007.

Cone, James. *The Cross and the Lynching Tree*. Maryknoll, NY: Orbis Books, 2011.

———. *The Spirituals and the Blues: An Interpretation*. Maryknoll, NY: Orbis Books, 1972.

Cooper, Stephen. *Augustine for Armchair Theologians*. Louisville: Westminster John Knox, 2002.

Crenshaw, Kimberlè. "Mapping the Margins: Intersectionality, Identity Politics, and Violence against Women of Color." *Stanford Law Review* 43, no.6 (July 1991): 1241–99.

———. "The Urgency of Intersectionality." Filmed October 2016 at TEDWomen 2016. TED video, 18:40. https://www.ted.com/talks/kimberle _crenshaw_the_urgency_of_intersectionality?language=en.

Crossan, John Dominic. *The Power of the Parable: How Fiction by Jesus Became Fiction about Jesus*. San Francisco: Harper, 2013.

Crowder, Stephanie Buckhanon. "Luke." In *True to Our Native Land: An African American New Testament Commentary*, edited by Brian K. Blount, Cain Hope Felder, Clarice J. Martin, and Emerson B. Powery, 158–85. Minneapolis: Fortress, 2007.

Dorrien, Gary. *The Making of American Liberal Theology: Idealism, Realism, and Modernity, 1900–1950*. Louisville: Westminster John Knox, 2003.

Douglass, Frederick. *My Bondage and My Freedom*. New York: Miller, Orton & Mulligan, 1855.

———. *Narrative of the Life of Frederick Douglass, an American Slave: Written by Himself*. Boston: Anti-Slavery Office, 1845.

Duckworth, Jessica Krey. *Wide Welcome: How the Unsettling Presence of Newcomers Can Save the Church*. Minneapolis: Fortress, 2013.

Duncan, Lenny. *Dear Church: A Love Letter from a Black Preacher to the Whitest Denomination in the U.S.* Minneapolis: Fortress, 2019.

Edwards, O. C. *Luke's Story of Jesus*. Philadelphia: Fortress, 1981.

Farrag, Hebah. "The Fight for Black Lives Is a Spiritual Movement." Berkley Forum, Berkley Center for Religion, Peace & World Affairs, Georgetown University, June 9, 2020. https://berkleycenter.georgetown.edu/responses/the-fight-for-black-lives-is-a-spiritual-movement.

Felder, Cain Hope. *Troubling Biblical Waters: Race, Class, and Family*. Maryknoll, NY: Orbis Books, 1989.

Ferrara Law Firm. "What You Need to Know about New Jersey's Good Samaritan Laws." The Ferrara Law Firm, posted March 16, 2018. https://ferraralawfirm.com/new-jerseys-good-samaritan-laws/.

Finkelstein, Lewis. *The Pharisees: The Sociological Background of Their Faith*. Philadelphia: Jewish Publication Society of America, 1938.

Fluker, Walter Earl, and Catherine Tumber, eds. *A Strange Freedom: The Best of Howard Thurman on Religious Experience and Public Life*. Boston: Beacon, 1998.

Fortin, Ernest L. Introduction to *Augustine: Political Writings*, by Augustine, vii–xxix. Edited by Ernest L. Fortin and Douglas Kries. Translated by Michael W. Tkacz and Douglas Kries. Indianapolis: Hackett, 1994.

Franklin, John Hope, and Alfred A. Moss Jr. *From Slavery to Freedom: A History of African Americans*. 8th ed. New York: Knopf, 2000.

Fredriksen, Paula. *Augustine and the Jews: A Christian Defense of Jews and Judaism.* New York: Doubleday, 2008.

Freedman, H., and M. Simon, eds. *Midrash Rabbah: Translated into English with Notes, Glossary, and Indices.* 10 vols. London: Soncino, 1939.

Fuller, Michael E. *Restoration of Israel: Israel's Re-gathering and the Fate of the Nations in Early Jewish Literature and Luke-Acts.* New York: de Gruyter, 2006.

Gafney, Wil. "A Reflection on the Black Lives Matter Movement and Its Impact on My Scholarship." *Journal of Biblical Literature* 136, no.1 (2017): 204–7.

Gowler, David B. *The Parables after Jesus: Their Imaginative Receptions across Two Millennia.* Grand Rapids: Baker Academic, 2017.

————. *What Are They Saying about the Parables?* New York: Paulist Press, 2000.

Green, Joel. *The Theology of the Gospel of Luke.* Cambridge: Cambridge University Press, 1995.

Grimké, Angelina. "An Appeal to the Christian Women of the South." In *Against Slavery: An Abolitionist Reader*, edited by Mason Lowance, 197–203. New York: Penguin Books, 2000.

Gullette, David, trans. *Nicaraguan Peasant Poetry from Solentiname.* Albuquerque: West End, 1988.

Harding, Vincent. Foreword to *Jesus and the Disinherited*, by Howard Thurman, v. 1949. Reprint, Boston: Beacon, 1996.

Harmless, William, ed. *Augustine in His Own Words.* Washington, DC: The Catholic University Press of America, 2010.

Hart, Drew G. I. *Who Will Be a Witness? Igniting Activism for God's Justice, Love, and Deliverance.* Harrisonburg, VA: Herald, 2020.

Hidalgo, Jacqueline M. "Scripturalizing the Pandemic." *Journal of Biblical Literature* 139, no. 3 (2020): 625–34.

Hughes, Langston. "Theme for English B," in *The Collected Works of Langston Hughes*, Vol. 3, *The Poems, 1951–1967*, edited by Arnold Rampersad, 51–52. Columbia: University of Missouri Press, 2001.

Itkowitz, Colby. "Her Son Shot Their Daughters 10 Years Ago. Then These Amish Families Embraced Her as a Friend." *Washington Post*, October 1, 2016. https://www.washingtonpost.com/news/inspired-life/wp/2016/10/01/10-years-ago-her-son-killed-amish-children-their-families-immediately-accepted-her-into-their-lives/?noredirect=on&utm_term=.3fc5ad64cea4.

Jacobs, Harriet Ann. *Incidents in the Life of a Slave Girl: Written by Herself*. Edited by L. Maria Child. Boston: Published for the Author, 1861.

———. "Letter from a Fugitive Slave." *New York Daily Tribune*, June 21, 1853, 6. https://docsouth.unc.edu/fpn/jacobs/support16.html.

Jones, Robert P. "Racism among White Christians Is Higher Than among the Nonreligious. That's No Coincidence." *Think: NBC News*, July 27, 2020. https://www.nbcnews.com/think/opinion/racism-among-white-christians-higher-among-nonreligious-s-no-coincidence-ncna1235045?cid=referral_taboolafeed.

Karris, Robert J. "The Gospel according to Luke." In *The New Jerome Biblical Commentary*, edited by Raymond E. Brown, Joseph A. Fitzmyer, and Roland E. Murphy, 675–721. Englewood Cliffs, NJ: Prentice Hall, 1990.

Keltner, Dacher. "The Compassionate Instinct." *Greater Good Magazine*, March 1, 2004. https://greatergood.berkeley.edu/article/item/the_compassionate_instinct.

King, Martin Luther, Jr. *Where Do We Go from Here: Chaos or Community?* Boston: Beacon, 1968.

Kraybill, Donald B., Steven M. Nolt, and David L. Weaver-Zercher. *Amish Grace: How Forgiveness Transcended Tragedy*. San Francisco: Jossey-Bass, 2007.

Leath, Jennifer S. "The Perpetual Cycle of However: Soul in the Fight for Racial Justice." Berkley Forum, Berkley Center for Religion, Peace & World Affairs, Georgetown University, June 22, 2020. https://berkleycenter.georgetown.edu/responses/the-perpetual-cycle-of-however-soul-in-the-fight-for-racial-justice.

Levenson, Jon. *The Resurrection and the Restoration of Israel*. New Haven: Yale University Press, 2006.

Levine, Amy-Jill. "The Disease of Postcolonial New Testament Studies and the Hermeneutics of Healing." *Journal of Feminist Studies in Religion* 20, no. 1 (Spring 2004): 91–132.

———. "Luke." In *The Jewish Annotated New Testament*, edited by Amy-Jill Levine and Marc Zvi Brettler, 107–67. Oxford: Oxford University Press, 2017.

———. *Short Stories by Jesus: The Enigmatic Parables of a Controversial Rabbi*. New York: HarperCollins, 2014.

Lewis, John. "Together, You Can Redeem the Soul of Our Nation." *The New York Times*, July 30, 2020. https://www.nytimes.com/2020/07/30 /opinion/john-lewis-civil-rights-america.html.

Lieu, Judith. *The Gospel of Luke*. Peterborough, UK: Epworth, 1997.

Liew, Benny. "Acts." In *Global Bible Commentary*, edited by Daniel Patte, 419–28. Nashville: Abingdon, 2004.

Lischer, Richard. *Reading the Parables*. Louisville: Westminster John Knox, 2014.

Longenecker, Bruce. "The Story of the Samaritan and the Innkeeper (Luke 10:30–35): A Study in Character Rehabilitation." *Biblical Interpretation* 17 (2009): 422–47.

M., Emelda. "Difference between Pity and Compassion." DifferenceBetween .net, April 27, 2011. http://www.differencebetween.net/science/nature /difference-between-pity-and-compassion/.

McKittrick, Katherine. *Demonic Grounds: Black Women and the Cartographies of Struggle*. Minneapolis: University of Minnesota Press, 2006.

Menéndez-Antuña, Luis. "Black Lives Matter and Gospel Hermeneutics: Political Life and Social Death in the Gospel of Luke." *Currents in Theology and Mission* 45, no. 4 (October 2018): 29–34.

Miller, Daniel. "Anti-Semitism Is on the Rise, 75 Years after the End of the Holocaust and Second World War." *The Conversation*, August 3, 2020. https://theconversation.com/anti-semitism-is-on-the-rise-75-years-after -the-end-of-the-holocaust-and-second-world-war-132141.

Morrison, Toni. *A Mercy*. New York: Knopf, 2008.

———. *The Origin of Others: The Charles Eliot Norton Lectures, 2016*. Cambridge, MA: Harvard University Press, 2017.

———. *Playing in the Dark: Whiteness and the Literary Imagination*. New York: Vintage Books, 1992.

Mosala, Itumeleng. *Biblical Hermeneutics and Black Theology in South Africa*. Grand Rapids: Eerdmans, 1989.

Nadella, Raj. *Dialogue Not Dogma: Many Voices in the Gospel of Luke*. Library of New Testament Studies 431. New York: T&T Clark, 2011.

Nahorniak, Mary. "Families to Roof: May God 'Have Mercy on Your Soul.'" *USA Today*, June 19, 2015. https://www.usatoday.com/story/news/2015 /06/19/bond-court-dylann-roof-charleston/28991607/.

Newton, Richard. "The African American Bible: Bound in a Christian Nation." *Journal of Biblical Literature* 136, no. 1 (2017): 221–28.

Nolland, John. *Luke 9:21–18:34*. Word Biblical Commentary 35B. Dallas: Word Books, 1993.

Northup, Solomon. *Twelve Years a Slave: Narrative of Solomon Northup, a Citizen of New York, Kidnapped in Washington City in 1841, and Rescued in 1853*. Auburn, NY: Derby and Miller, 1853.

O'Connor, Kathleen. *Jeremiah: Pain and Promise*. Minneapolis: Fortress, 2011.

Oppenheimer, Mark. "Some Evangelicals Struggle with Black Lives Matter Movement." *Sojourners*. Accessed August 27, 2020. https://sojo.net/about-us/news/some-evangelicals-struggle-black-lives-matter-movement.

Powell, Mark Allan. *Introducing the New Testament: A Historical, Literary, and Theological Survey*. Grand Rapids: Baker Academic, 2018.

Powery, Emerson B. "'Rise Up, Ye Women': Harriet Jacobs and the Bible." *Postscripts: The Journal of Sacred Texts, Cultural Histories, and Contemporary Contexts* 5, no. 2 (2009): 171–84.

————. "Tax Collector." In *The New Interpreter's Dictionary of the Bible*, edited by Katharine Doob Sakenfeld, 5:477–78. Nashville: Abingdon, 2009.

Powery, Emerson B., and Rodney S. Sadler. *The Genesis of Liberation: Biblical Interpretation in the Antebellum Narratives of the Enslaved*. Louisville: Westminster John Knox, 2016.

Powery, Luke A., and Emerson B. Powery. "King, the Bible, and the 'World House': A Visionary Critique of the American Bible." In *The Word Made Flesh: Biblical Rhetoric in the Speeches and Sermons of Martin Luther King, Jr.*, edited by Herbert Marbury, Love Sechrest, and Lewis Baldwin. Columbia: University of South Carolina Press, forthcoming.

Pummer, Reinhard. *The Samaritans: A Profile*. Grand Rapids: Eerdmans, 2016.

Reed, Jean-Pierre. "The Bible, Religious Storytelling, and Revolution: The Case of Solentiname, Nicaragua." *Critical Research on Religion* 5, no. 3 (2017): 227–50.

Ringe, Sharon H. *Luke*. Louisville: Westminster John Knox, 1995.

Sack, Kevin, and Alan Blinder. "Heart-Rending Testimony as Dylann Roof Trial Opens." *New York Times*, December 7, 2016. https://www.nytimes.com/2016/12/07/us/dylann-roof-trial.html.

Sanders, Cheryl J. "Do Black Lives Matter to God? Reflections on History, Theology, and Hope amid the Flames of Outrage." Berkley Forum, Berkley Center for Religion, Peace & World Affairs, Georgetown University, June 17, 2020. https://berkleycenter.georgetown.edu/responses/do-black

-lives-matter-to-god-reflections-on-history-theology-and-hope-amid-the
-flames-of-outrage.

Sanders, Jack T. *The Jews in Luke-Acts.* Philadelphia: Fortress, 1987.

Santamarina, Xiomara. "Black Womanhood in North American Women's
Slave Narratives." In *The Cambridge Companion to the African American
Slave Narrative,* edited by Audrey Fisch, 232–45. Cambridge: Cambridge
University Press, 2007.

Sawyer, Sam. "Who Became a Neighbor? Reading Black Lives Matter
through the Good Samaritan." *America: The Jesuit Review,* July 10,
2016. https://www.americamagazine.org/politics-society/2016/07/10/who
-became-neighbor-reading-black-lives-matter-through-good-samaritan.

Schaberg, Jane D., and Sharon H. Ringe. "Gospel of Luke." In *Women's Bible
Commentary,* 20th anniv. ed., edited by Carol A. Newsom, Sharon H.
Ringe, and Jacqueline E. Lapsley, 493–511. Louisville: Westminster John
Knox, 2012.

Scharper, Philip, and Sally Scharper, eds. *The Gospel in Art by the Peasants
of Solentiname.* Maryknoll, NY: Orbis Books, 1984.

Schiffman, Lawrence. "The Samaritans in Tannaitic Halakhah." *Jewish
Quarterly Review* 75 (1985): 323–50.

Schottroff, Luise. *The Parables of Jesus.* Translated by Linda M. Maloney.
Minneapolis: Fortress, 2006.

Sechrest, Love L. *A Former Jew: Paul and the Dialectics of Race.* London:
T&T Clark, 2009.

Smith, Luther. Foreword to *Sermons on the Parables,* by Howard Thurman,
xi–xiv. Edited by David B. Gowler and Kipton E. Jenson. Maryknoll, NY:
Orbis Books, 2018.

Snodgrass, Klyne. *Stories with Intent: A Comprehensive Guide to the Parables of Jesus.* 2nd ed. Grand Rapids: Eerdmans, 2018.

Stark, Judith Chelius. "Augustine on Women: In God's Image, but Less So."
In Stark, *Feminist Interpretations of Augustine,* 215–42.

———, ed. *Feminist Interpretations of Augustine.* University Park: Penn
State University Press, 2007.

Stave, Shirley A. "'More Sinned against Than Sinning': Redefining Sin and
Redemption in *Beloved* and *A Mercy.*" In *Contested Boundaries: New
Critical Essays on the Fiction of Toni Morrison,* edited by Maxine L.
Montgomery, 126–41. Newcastle upon Tyne, UK: Cambridge Scholars,
2013.

Teske, Roland. "The Good Samaritan (Lk 10:29–37) in Augustine's Exegesis." In *Augustine: Biblical Exegete*, edited by Frederick Van Fleteren and Joseph C. Schnaubelt, 347–67. New York: Peter Lang, 2001.

Theissen, Gerd. *The Shadow of the Galilean*. Philadelphia: Fortress, 1987.

Thurman, Howard. *Deep Is the Hunger*. 1951. Reprint, Richmond, IN: Friends United, 2000.

———. "Forgiveness: The Two Debtors (Luke 7:36–50) and the Unmerciful Servant (Matthew 18:23–25)." In *Sermons on the Parables*, 37–46.

———. "The Good Samaritan (Luke 10:25–37)." In *Sermons on the Parables*, 47–56.

———. *Jesus and the Disinherited*. 1949. Reprint, Boston: Beacon, 1996.

———. *Sermons on the Parables*. Edited by David B. Gowler and Kipton E. Jenson. Maryknoll, NY: Orbis Books, 2018.

———. *With Head and Heart: The Autobiography of Howard Thurman*. San Diego: Harcourt, Brace & Company, 1979.

Tinsley, Cleve V., IV. "Amid Phantoms of Death: A Call for New Paradigms of Religious Response to Uprisings for Black Lives." Berkley Forum, Berkley Center for Religion, Peace & World Affairs, Georgetown University, June 18, 2020. https://berkleycenter.georgetown.edu/responses/amid-phantoms-of-death-a-call-for-new-paradigms-of-religious-response-to-uprisings-for-black-lives.

"Toni Morrison Discusses *A Mercy*." NPR, October 29, 2008. YouTube video, 9:56. https://www.youtube.com/watch?v=7IZvMhQ2LIU.

Toussaint, Loren L., Everett L. Worthington, and David R. Williams, eds. *Forgiveness and Health: Scientific Evidence and Theories Relating Forgiveness to Better Health*. New York: Springer, 2015.

Tutu, Desmond. *No Future without Forgiveness*. London: Rider Books, 1999.

———. "Truth and Reconciliation Commission, South Africa." In *Encyclopedia Britannica*. Article published April 6, 2010; last modified February 4, 2019. https://www.britannica.com/topic/Truth-and-Reconciliation-Commission-South-Africa.

Vinson, Richard B. *Luke*. Macon, GA: Smyth & Helwys, 2008.

Walker, Christina. "10 Years. 180 School Shootings. 356 Victims." CNN. 2019. https://www.cnn.com/interactive/2019/07/us/ten-years-of-school-shootings-trnd/.

Webb, Samuel, ed. "Speech of Angelina E. G. Weld." In *History of Pennsylvania Hall Which Was Destroyed by a Mob on the 17th of May, 1838*, 123–26. New York: Negro Universities Press, 1969.

Willard, Mara. "Interrogating *A Mercy*: Faith, Fiction, and the Postsecular." *Christianity and Literature* 63, no. 4 (2014): 467–87.

Williams, Demetrius. "The Acts of the Apostles." In *True to Our Native Land*, edited by Brian K. Blount, Cain Hope Felder, Clarice J. Martin, and Emerson B. Powery, 213–48. Minneapolis: Fortress, 2007.

Wills, Lawrence. "Mark." In *The Jewish Annotated New Testament*, edited by Amy-Jill Levine and Marc Zvi Brettler, 67–106. New York: Oxford University Press, 2017.

Yellin, Jean Fagan. *Harriet Jacobs: A Life*. Cambridge, MA: Basic Civitas Books, 2004.

———, ed. *The Harriet Jacobs Family Papers*. Vol. 1. Chapel Hill: University of North Carolina Press, 2008.

———. "Texts and Contexts of Harriet Jacobs' *Incidents in the Life of a Slave Girl: Written by Herself*." In *The Slave's Narrative*, edited by Charles T. Davis and Henry Louis Gates Jr., 262–82. Oxford: Oxford University Press, 1985.

Young, Josiah U., III. "'Many Thousands Gone': Theology, Race, and Justice." Berkley Forum, Berkley Center for Religion, Peace & World Affairs, Georgetown University, June 15, 2020. https://berkleycenter.georgetown.edu/responses/many-thousands-gone-theology-race-and-justice.

Scripture Index

Subject Index